Pleasure

Also by Hilda Hutcherson, M.D.

*What Your Mother Never Told
You About S-e-x*

Pleasure

A Woman's Guide to Getting the Sex You Want, Need, and Deserve

Hilda Hutcherson, M.D.

G. P. PUTNAM'S SONS / NEW YORK

G. P. PUTNAM'S SONS
Publishers Since 1838
Published by the Penguin Group
Penguin Group (USA) Inc., 375 Hudson Street, New York, New York 10014, USA • Penguin Group (Canada),
90 Eglinton Avenue East, Suite 700, Toronto, Ontario M4P 2Y3, Canada (a division of Pearson Penguin Canada
Inc.) • Penguin Books Ltd, 80 Strand, London WC2R 0RL, England • Penguin Ireland, 25 St Stephen's Green,
Dublin 2, Ireland (a division of Penguin Books Ltd) • Penguin Group (Australia), 250 Camberwell Road,
Camberwell, Victoria 3124, Australia (a division of Pearson Australia Group Pty Ltd) • Penguin Books India Pvt
Ltd, 11 Community Centre, Panchsheel Park, New Delhi–110 017, India • Penguin Group (NZ), Cnr Airborne
and Rosedale Roads, Albany, Auckland 1310, New Zealand (a division of Pearson New Zealand Ltd) • Penguin
Books (South Africa) (Pty) Ltd, 24 Sturdee Avenue, Rosebank, Johannesburg 2196, South Africa

Penguin Books Ltd, Registered Offices:
80 Strand, London WC2R 0RL, England

Library of Congress Cataloging-in-Publication Data

Hutcherson, Hilda.
Pleasure: a woman's guide to getting the sex you want, need, and deserve / Hilda Hutcherson.
p. cm.
Includes bibliographical references and index.
ISBN 0-399-15304-7
1. Sex instruction for women.   2. Women—Sexual behavior.   3. Sex.   4. Pleasure.   I. Title.
HQ46.H836   2006   2005050987
613.9'6—dc22

Printed in the United States of America
1   3   5   7   9   10   8   6   4   2

Book design by Lovedog Studio

While the author has made every effort to provide accurate telephone numbers and Internet addresses at the time of
publication, neither the publisher nor the author assumes any responsibility for errors, or for changes that occur after
publication. Further, the publisher does not have any control over and does not assume any responsibility for author
or third-party websites or their content.

Neither the publisher nor the author is engaged in rendering professional advice or services to the individual reader.
The ideas, procedures, and suggestions contained in this book are not intended as a substitute for consulting with
your physician. All matters regarding your health require medical supervision. Neither the author nor the publisher
shall be liable or responsible for any loss or damage allegedly arising from any information or suggestion in this book.

This book is dedicated to my sister, Synitra Hutcherson, who has always encouraged me to live life to its fullest. I love you, Sis.

Acknowledgments

This book would not have been possible without the support of many people.

Thanks to the following writers, physicians, and friends for their assistance, comments, and expert advice: Sharon Boone; Monique Brown; Anette Candido; Robert Corbellini; Sharon Grotevant; Rachel Grumman; Cynthia Henderson; Gerald Hoke, M.D.; Synitra Hutcherson; Nancy Jasper, M.D.; Elana Katz, M.S.W.; Dawn Kum Walks; Amy Levine; Roger Lobo, M.D.; Barbara Miller; JoAnn Perrino; Gene Pope; Ridwan Shabsigh, M.D.; Holly Taylor; and my students at Columbia University College of Physicians and Surgeons, who cheered me on.

My sincere thanks to Tamara Jeffries, a very gifted writer and editor, who was always available to read, comment, and advise.

Thank you to my incredible agent of ten years, Carla Glasser, and my talented illustrator, Judith Cummins. A million thanks to my fabulous editor, Marian Lizzi, for her unwavering support and encouragement.

And, as always, a special thank-you to my husband, Fredric Fabiano, and my children, Lauren, Steven, Andrew, and Freddie. Thank you for your understanding and love.

A final thank-you to the thousands of women to whom I have had the honor of speaking in the last few years. Thank you for your stories and for sharing your wisdom. Thank you for allowing me to be a member of the sisterhood.

Contents

IV. Kicking It Up a Notch

V. Adding Some Extra Spice

VI. A Lifetime of Pleasure

Introduction

Great sex. It makes us feel good physically, emotionally, and even spiritually. I believe it's what every woman and man deserves. Besides all the obvious reasons to love intimate, satisfying sex—and to define it and seek it out for ourselves—there's now evidence that it can even prolong our lives. A recent study published in the *British Medical Journal* found that men who had frequent orgasms had half the risk of dying from heart disease and other causes than men with fewer orgasms.[1] Other studies have shown that while the number of sexual encounters is most important in men, the *quality* of sex, or sexual satisfaction, is more important in women's health and longevity.[2] Still another study showed that sexual *dissatisfaction* may be a risk factor

[1] Smith, G. "Sex and Death: Are they related? Findings from the Caerphilly Cohort Study," *BMJ* 315 (20 December): 1641–44.
[2] Palnore, E. "Predictors of the longevity difference: a 25-year follow-up," *Gerontologist* 6 (1982): 513–18.

for heart disease in women.[3] Satisfying sex decreases stress and anxiety, improves sleep, and just plain makes you feel good and alive. In other words, it puts a smile on your face.

In the years since publication of my first book, *What Your Mother Never Told You About S-e-x*, I have traveled the country speaking to women about the importance of mutually satisfying sex. On these trips as well as in my practice as a gynecologist and in my work as a contributing editor and columnist for *Glamour* and *Essence* magazines, I get hundreds of questions from women about sex and sexual health. I wrote *What Your Mother Never Told You About S-e-x* because so many women had questions about their own sexual anatomy and sexual technique. Some women I encountered admitted to having only the most basic, perfunctory information about sex even though many had been having sex for years. That first book provided the basic information about "plumbing" and positions, and answered some fundamental questions. But once we'd covered that ground, I discovered that women still craved more information.

While many women across America are having plenty of sex, many aren't experiencing the level of *pleasure* they'd like to feel. They want sex that's more than just the union of two bodies. They want to come away from the experience feeling satisfied, glowing with contentment. They want to experience a more complete sense of pleasure, not just good sex but great, *satisfying* sex. And as I've listened to thousands of women who have shared their stories with me, one thing always intrigued me: The definition and experience of pleasure of every one of these women are different.

Many women have written to me and expressed feelings of sexual inadequacy. Most of these feelings stem from the tremendous pressure that women feel to perform in bed. They're not comfortable unless their bodies look a certain way. They feel they should be hav-

[3]Abramov, L. "Sexual life and frigidity among women developing acute myocardial infarction," *Psychosomatic Medicine* 38 (1976): 418–25.

ing orgasms—better yet, multiple orgasms—every time. They feel they're supposed to know every position, every technique, and every trick that will make their partner climb the walls. When the sexual experience does not measure up to this ideal, some women—or their partners—are left feeling unfulfilled and inadequate.

My message is this: Pleasure is not about performance and goals. How can you have the joyful experience of pleasure if you're judging yourself, worrying about your partner, or counting orgasms? Pleasure comes when you're relaxed, when you're comfortable with yourself and your partner, and with what you're doing together. Pleasure is exciting and exhilarating. It's thrilling. And it's as individual as you are. There is no one right way to achieve pleasure. You define your own pleasure—hopefully for yourself—and seek it out and enjoy it to the fullest.

This book has been written to give you steps on the pathway to pleasure. The first step is to become an authority on your own body. That means learning, and appreciating, all of your unique body parts and how they work. Only when you learn to love and honor your genitals and the rest of your body will you be able to abandon yourself to the erotic sensations—emotional and physical—of sex. When you feel good about your physical self, you can throw off the covers, turn on the lights, and gaze into your partner's eyes as your bodies join in ecstasy.

You deserve, and should feel entitled to, sexual pleasure. Many of us have not reached our sexual potential because we are not sure what exactly we want or need to be sexually satisfied. Too often we wait for our partners to provide us with just the right stimulation, the magic touch. You must take responsibility for your own pleasure. In order to achieve the sex that you deserve, you must go on a journey of self-discovery. It is essential that you explore and identify what makes *you* feel good. Once you discover what turns you on, you must feel deserving enough to share that information with your partner. After all, most of our partners really do want to know what makes us happy. In my travels, many men have asked me to tell them what women really want in bed. Communication with your partner is one of the most important keys to sexual satisfaction. In Part II, I provide instructions on how to become confident in your sexuality, discover what you want, and communicate those desires to your partner.

To have the ultimate sexual experience, you must allow yourself to accept as well as give pleasure. As women, we often find it much easier to give than to receive. We are much more comfortable in our roles as caregivers, taking care of someone else's needs. Relaxing, receiving, and letting go may be the most difficult part of sex for some of us. In Part III, I present steps to take on your journey to becoming a woman who is free and open to receiving pleasure.

Sexual techniques and skills are important—and more than 150 tips and techniques are provided in Part III—but sex is more than two bodies going through a series of positions and movements. The emotional experience of sex is equally important. For many women, closeness, intimacy, and spiritual connection are the most satisfying aspects of sex. Each person brings unique feelings and emotions to the encounter. Understanding your feelings as well as those of your partner increases the intimacy and spiritual connection that elevates good sex to great sex. In this book, I discuss the psychological and emotional components that may affect the sexual experience for men and women.

In the best of relationships, sex can become stale and lifeless. The key is to constantly add spice and interest to your sex life. Part IV shows you how to kick it up a notch, with more than fifty tips to increase your pleasure. Orgasm is only one of many possible sources of sexual pleasure. This section discusses how to increase the chance that you will experience an orgasm—whether it be your first or your millionth—and, more important, that it will be truly satisfying.

Sexual pleasure is important throughout your lifetime, though it may change as you go through life's phases. Perhaps the most surprising and alarming change for women occurs after marriage, when the frequency and intensity of sex often decrease. And having children, no matter how much you adore them, creates new obstacles for intimacy. Menopause adds yet another set of challenges to the pursuit of sexual pleasure. Tips on how to keep your sex life hot and exciting forever are presented in Part VI.

In my travels, many women have asked me to write a "spicier" sequel to *What Your Mother Never Told You About S-e-x. Pleasure* is my answer to those requests. It has been a labor of love, and I hope you enjoy reading it as much as I have enjoyed writing it. I wish you joy, happiness, excitement, satisfaction, and a lifetime of pleasure.

I

. . . . .

In Pursuit
of Pleasure

1
. . . . .

Pleasure Principles

Pleasure. The word itself brings a smile to your face. Your mind turns to memories of time spent with someone you care about, a place you love, or an occasion that brought you joy. You may remember drinking hot cocoa after a day of playing in the snow. Going dancing with close friends. Walking along the beach on your honeymoon. Your child's first laugh. A wonderful Thanksgiving meal with family. Shopping for a glorious new pair of shoes. Or sitting alone on a peaceful evening, watching the sun set over the hills.

Pleasure takes many forms. Of course, in my line of work, when I hear the word *pleasure* I immediately think of sexual pleasure. But even sexual pleasure isn't one thing. It includes a spectrum of feelings from sweet, simple satisfaction to utter, indescribable bliss. For some people, pleasure is the familiar embrace of a lover who knows your every curve and quirk. Others aren't happy unless they're tingling with sexual excitement, weak-kneed and breathless; their pleasure is heightened with new partners, new positions, new experiences and experiments. Pleasure is different—completely, mysteriously, deliciously different—for each person.

And that's the beauty of sexual pleasure. But it can also be the challenge for those of us seeking our own sexual nirvana: Your best friend can tell you her surefire secret to sensual bliss, but it may not work for you at all. You could try to replicate the steamiest scene in the sexiest movie and find that it just feels ridiculous when it's you and your husband, instead of two young movie stars. Even your beloved's idea of an exciting coupling could leave you cold.

Don't be discouraged. Regardless of your age, sexual history, inhibitions, and other concerns, you can have the sex you desire. You're not going to find it by asking around. You're not even going to find it in this book—at least not in the way you might think. You can only discover sexual pleasure by getting intimate with your own body, releasing your inhibitions about sex, learning what feels good and what doesn't (and communicating that with your partner), and opening your mind and heart as well as your body to the possibility of pleasure. It's all about *you*. This book is going to guide you along the path to discovering sexual pleasure, but the exploration and experimentation will be for you to do. This journey will be yours to take, and the bliss you find will be your own to share and enjoy throughout your lifetime. (By the way, what is pleasurable to you now may change over the course of your life. The good news is that once you know how to find it, you'll always know how to get there.)

It is important to also be aware that there will be times in your life when sex will not be great. Your desire for sex may go downhill or you may find it difficult to become aroused. Your vagina may not lubricate the way you like or you may have difficulty achieving the level of sexual pleasure to which you have become accustomed, or to which you aspire. You may have pain and completely lose your interest in sex, either alone or with a partner. Sexual problems may be caused by medical problems, medications, and relationship problems with your mate. The good news is that help exists for almost any sexual problem or dysfunction. For a complete discussion of sexual dysfunction, see *What Your Mother Never Told You About S-e-x.*

Body and Soul

You might think of a sex book as the equivalent of a plumbing manual. Indeed many such books are all about body parts and positions. They have to be—at least to an extent—because you can't know how to get the sexual pleasure you desire unless you first know how your body functions. So we will review anatomy in the pages that follow. Your body is an important part of your sexual experience. *An* important part but not the *only* important part. Not even the *most* important part. Sexual pleasure is far more complex than the joining of genitals. True pleasure is an experience of your mind and your emotions as much as it is of your body.

First of all, plant firmly in your mind the idea that you *deserve* pleasure. Repeat after me: *I deserve to have pleasure in my life. I deserve all kinds of pleasant, joyful experiences, including sexual experiences.* Keep saying it to yourself until you believe it. If that mantra doesn't work, do whatever you must to convince yourself to the very core of your being that you deserve pleasure. You're not going to have the kinds of sexual experiences you want until you wrap your mind around the idea that pleasure is your right. Too many of us accept an "okay" sex life, as if that's the best we can hope for and the most we are worthy of. Okay sex is better than bad sex, right? So we should be satisfied with that, shouldn't we? Well, "yes" to the first question; "no" to the last. Okay sex *is* better than bad sex, but why should you be satisfied with lovemaking that's just "okay" when you have the potential for so much more? You do deserve to have a love life that's fun, gratifying, tender, passionate, thrilling . . . whatever you dream it can be. And believing that you're worth the effort is the first step to getting there. It might take a little practice, some talking, some time, but you can have the love life you want. And you should.

Some of us feel that we deserve good sex but can't quite seem to enjoy it, because we're too caught up in our deep-seated notions of what we should and shouldn't do. Even while we're having sex, deep in the back of our minds, we're remembering negative sexual messages that have been passed down to us. We're envisioning the disapproval of our parents. We're transported back to high school, when having sex meant risking being labeled a slut. So many messages we receive indicate that sex is bad; it may take practice to envision it as something good.

Back in the sixties, we talked about "free love." Love is only free if your mind is free. As you read the pages that follow, I want you to open your mind and begin to toss away the mental blocks that might be keeping you from truly enjoying your love life. Those blockages might include guilt, fear, or false expectations. Maybe you're holding on to resentments or anger with your current partner or partners past. If you've had particularly negative sexual experiences—something that hurt you physically or emotionally—you may have a difficult time opening up to the idea of great sex. You will need to work through that tangle of emotions in order to truly free yourself to have the kind of love life you desire.

Sex is often better if you're emotionally involved. You can have fabulous sex with someone you like and are attracted to or even with some hottie you just met (and that's okay). When your partner is truly your *lover*—a person who loves you and in whom you are emotionally invested—wonderful sex soars to the level of the sublime. I'm not saying that you can't have satisfying sex unless you're with the love of your life, but, like it or not, sex does involve our emotions. And when those feelings are positive ones—when you feel safe, honored, complete, and confident—the quality of sex increases. You can find more pleasure in the experience if you're able to open your heart to whomever you are sharing your body with.

In fact, some people believe that if you take sex beyond the physical, it can be elevated to the level of a spiritual experience. But that's nothing new. In many ancient cultures, including Egypt, Mesopotamia, and India, sex was often celebrated as a magical, mystical act and was incorporated into spiritual ceremonies. Sex was honored and revered instead of feared and shunned. Over time, and particularly in the West, the relationship between sex and spirituality has become a distant one. But I do believe that sexual practice can be a beautiful sharing of spirit and the spiritual union between two people. It certainly can't hurt to approach sex that way. You may find that it helps you discover the ultimate sexual pleasure.

Giving and Getting

Sexual pleasure is a two-way street: You have to be able to give pleasure as well as receive it. When we're talking about sex, that might seem obvious, but for many people it's a difficult path to follow.

For women, the issue is quite often that we can't allow ourselves to open up and accept pleasure. Some of us can't even accept a compliment. Think about it: When someone tells us that he or she likes our hair or our shoes, instead of smiling and being pleased, we deflect the compliment and start to find fault with that or some other aspect of ourselves. If you can't accept the simple pleasure of someone's admiration, you might also find yourself unconsciously deflecting opportunities for the deeper pleasure of intimacy. In the same way we have to train ourselves to accept a compliment, accept help, accept any gift we're being offered, we also have to learn to open up to accept pleasure as a well-deserved part of our lives. Don't ever turn it away.

Many of us are in the habit of putting other people first and accepting the leftovers for ourselves. That applies to sex as well. We have sex when our partner suggests it, we do it the way our partner likes it, and once we make sure our partner is completely satisfied, it's over. But sometimes you have to *ask for what you want* in life as well as in sex. Don't wait for someone to guess what you desire. Talk about it with your partner, tell him what pleases you, and ask him to do the things you like. And spend some time together discovering new avenues to mutual pleasure.

Of course, some of us are so eager in our pursuit of orgasm and sexual ecstasy that we forget that our sexual experiences are something we're sharing with a partner. While I believe a woman should have all the pleasure she can stand, she should also remember that sex is a partnership and that good sex means both partners come away glowing with pleasure. Do you want him to perform oral sex on you? Then offer *him* oral sex once in a while. Like to be touched or kissed a certain way? Demonstrate on him, then find out what he likes. Try the positions he finds exciting. Act out one of his fantasies. You might be surprised at how much it turns you on to turn him on.

Being able to give and receive pleasure is important even when you are pleasuring yourself. Though we as a society are beginning to accept self-pleasuring as part of a healthy sex life, many of us still feel uncomfortable with the idea. It's important to be able to give yourself pleasure—whatever that means for you—and open yourself up to enjoy it. Self-pleasuring may take many forms, all of them personal and private. We most often think of masturbating, but we may also pleasure ourselves by using sex toys or fantasizing. Or consider the sensuous (but not necessarily sexual) pleasure of giving yourself time to indulge in a warm, scented bath, allowing the water to envelop and lap against your body. (A removable showerhead or strategically placed whirlpool jets may take your private bath to another level of pleasure.) You may enjoy the sensuality of stripping off your tight, binding, uncomfortable clothes; allowing yourself to walk around in the nude; letting your skin breathe and enjoying reflections of your beautiful naked body as you pass a mirror. Or just ditch the panties sometimes; spend your day wearing nothing under your clothes. Taking time to do anything that you find sensuous is the first step to self-pleasuring. Be willing to give yourself that private, intimate time and be willing to enjoy it without reservation.

Chasing Orgasm

When you ask people how they define good sex, many will include in their description a satisfying climax. Orgasm. The Big O. That's what sex is all about, isn't it? Actually, I don't believe orgasm is the best indicator of great sex. You can have intense, even multiple orgasms without feeling satisfied. And you can experience blissful, breathtaking, satisfying sex without reaching climax. In fact you can have good sex without ever having communion of the genitals. (More on that later.)

Today, for many women (and men), female orgasm has become the holy grail of sex. Many people feel that if you don't have one, you haven't had good sex. Unfortunately, we sometimes take it beyond simple disappointment; we elevate it to the level of a personal failure. We think something is wrong with us. We blame our bodies; we blame ourselves. Many of us feel inadequate if we don't have an orgasm—or multiple orgasms—every time we have sex. Too often, we put ourselves through all sorts of negative feelings—disappointment, anger, resentment, fear—for lack of a few moments of sexual climax.

It's not that I don't want you to have orgasms as many and as often as you like. And if you have difficulty coming to climax, I hope the exercises in this book will help you. You may find that reaching orgasm will be simply a matter of finding the right position, discovering what kind of stimulation turns you on, adding a little sex play or fantasy to help things along. You may have to try different things to see what works for you. We'll work on that in the pages that follow. But at the same time, I am offering a piece of advice that might seem completely counterintuitive: *Don't chase orgasm. Let orgasm come to you.* Yes, try different positions, learn and practice new techniques, communicate with your partner. But please do everything you can to keep from entering each sexual encounter with the pressure of having an orgasm hanging over your bed. Don't allow that to be the goal of your sexual experience; don't let that be your *only* definition of pleasure. When you have sex, enjoy yourself: touch your partner and let him touch you, kiss passionately, wrap your bodies around each other, get into it totally and completely. Live in the moment. Forget about everything else. Focus on the wonderful physical and emotional sensations you are experiencing. And when the moment ends, if you've experienced an orgasm, that's great. If you haven't had an orgasm, you've still had great sex and you can look forward to the next wonderful opportunity for pleasure.

I know a woman who had wonderful sex for years. She enjoyed herself and she let her partners know it, but she never had orgasms. She assumed she couldn't have them during intercourse. (As is the case with many women, she could have them when she masturbated.) Then one day, in the throes of making love with her partner—a man she'd been intimate with for a long time—she began to feel something different happening. The rhythm of their movements, their position, the passion with which he approached her—it all came together for her, and she had a powerful, thrilling orgasm. She was shocked; so was her partner. Needless to say, they were both delighted. And now she knew what she needed to have orgasm: how long it took, what position she needed to be in, what part of her body responded to which kind of stimulation.

The point here is that this young woman wasn't *trying* to have an orgasm. Her partner wasn't pressuring her. She was enjoying herself just fine without it. And as she became comfortable with her body and with her partner, orgasm just found its way into her life. Often, that's how it works. The better you know your desires, your body, and your sexual preferences—and the more comfortable you are with your sexuality in general and the specific sexual situation you're in—the more likely you are to encourage orgasm into your sex life. But when you focus on racing toward the goal of orgasm, you may ignore the sensual experience of the journey and rob yourself of the true pleasure of sex.

To achieve the ultimate pleasure, focus on enjoying all of the physical and emotional sensations that you and your partner create when you're together. Savor his scent, the feeling of his skin against yours, the movement of energy from his body to yours and back again. Relax and allow orgasm to come to you if it wishes. But always remember that orgasm is just one of many potential sources of sexual pleasure.

Sensual, Scintillating, Not-Quite Sex

Not only can you have great sex without orgasm, you can have great sex . . . *without having sex.* Stay with me here. First, you have to understand that I define *sex* as any number of sensual experiences between two people, including but not limited to intercourse. The joining of genitals is just one way to be intimate. But think about it: There's sexual touching, oral sex, phone sex, fantasies—all kinds of ways to have a great time sexually. In fact, some women have told me that the most pleasurable experience they've had sexually did not include intercourse. Take this scenario that a woman shared with me:

His hands stroked the back of my ear, slid down my cheek, and lingered at my lips. His fingers traced each soft curve as he told me how much he loved my lips—my plump, pouting mouth. My lips parted slightly to accept the tip of his pinky, but his fingers continued along the curve of my neck to my collarbone and then down toward my breasts. I tensed. My breasts were not as firm as they once were, and my belly was etched with stretch marks, souvenirs of childbirth. But he stood back and looked at my naked form hungrily. "You are the most beautiful woman I have ever seen," he told me. And I felt my body relax. I sighed. For the next four hours—four hours!—we kissed, cuddled, touched, stroked, massaged, explored, and laughed. No intercourse. No pressure to perform. It was the most pleasurable experience of my entire life.

If you come away from an encounter with your lover feeling the way this woman did—satisfied and basking in the afterglow—who says traditional intercourse needs to be part of it? I want you to be able to think about your intimate life, your romantic life, your life of pleasure without attaching it to intercourse. That way you can find a multitude of ways to share intimacy—and pleasure—with your partner.

And think about it: Isn't it better to have more ways to enjoy sex than fewer? You want your partner to be able to make love to your knees, your hair, the nape of your neck, your freckles, your dimples, your feet. You want to be able to kiss, as one woman put it, "until I thought my lips were going to fall off." Or to touch each other everywhere—until you both reach the highest summits of pleasure. And if the experience goes no further, you will still be able to say "Wow, we had great sex last night."

Write Your Own Script

I've written this book to help guide you toward sexual pleasure, but the truth is that you have to write your own script. You'll find techniques, positions, exercises, games, toys, all kinds of suggestions, and ideas to try. But in the end, the combination of techniques and practices you incorporate into your sex life will be as individual as you are.

Don't try to keep up with the Joneses. First of all, unless you're peeping into their bedroom, you have no idea what their sex life is really like, no matter how passionately, how often, or how intensely they *say* they're coupling. No one's sex life is perfect, day in and day out for years at a time, not even the Joneses'. Don't try to measure your sex life against someone else's.

At some point you're going to read a statistic that says the "average" person has sex x number of times per week, and I'll bet that x is not going to match up with how often you engage in intercourse. The averages are just abstract numbers; they don't have any real bearing on your life. What matters is whether or not you are happy with the quality and quantity of sex in your life.

As a final note, for goodness sake, please don't use the movies, the soaps, romance novels, or late-night television shows as an indicator of what sex should be like. Real sex involves real people. And that means wrinkles and love handles, stretch marks and cellulite. It means that sometimes you won't feel like having sex at all: You'll be angry or grieving, or too busy or distracted or stressed. And sometimes you'll be powerfully in the mood, but your partner won't be. And in real life, even with all those obstacles, you can still have a delicious sex life. You can have all the pleasure you desire. You deserve it. You can orchestrate it for yourself. Now let's see how.

2
. . . . .

Your Body: Female Sexual Anatomy

You probably take it for granted. Your body is just . . . your body. You probably don't think about it much unless it starts to complain: *My back is killing me. When did these crow's-feet crop up? Why do they call these things love handles? I hate them.* And even when your body is perhaps most fully engaged—when you're having sex—you're probably thinking more about whether he's noticing your dimply thighs or your too-small breasts than about how magnificent a creation you are.

If you stop to think about your body more objectively, you'll be amazed to realize just how ideally it is designed to give you pleasure. Almost every body part, from the lobe of your ear to the inside of your thigh, can be kissed or caressed in a way that causes you to melt with pleasure. Your body is one big erogenous zone. What's not to love about that?

To fully enjoy sex, it is essential that you get to know your body better. You and your partner need to know your anatomy, how it functions, and what feels good where. And I'm talking about your whole body: your sexual anatomy, yes, but also parts of your body you don't think of as erogenous zones. Each part of your body is beautiful and capable of providing pleasurable sensations. Learning more about your body will enhance your sexual confidence and satisfaction as well, because you'll be able to tell your partner (or show him) exactly what to touch, exactly how to touch it, and exactly how wonderful it feels.

In this chapter, I'm going to give you a road map for exploring your anatomy, especially your sexual anatomy. (Though I should warn you that I have a very broad definition of what a sex organ is.) But remember that *you* are the one who is going on the journey. Because your body is absolutely unlike any other on the planet—with its own shape, size, and responses—this will be a unique process of exploration and discovery for you. I'll tell you what's what and what's where, but as you begin to look and touch and try new things, you'll discover a whole new you: your sensual, sexual self.

I recommend you explore a little on your own first, but you shouldn't hesitate to invite your partner to join you in exploration when you're ready. The person you make love with will surely benefit from knowing as much as possible about your body. And his sexual knowledge can only be a benefit to you.

The Sum of Your Parts

Many women refer to their sexual anatomy as "down there" or "down below" as if it's one vague region. In fact, "down there" is a complex, delightfully intricate and fascinating place. Let's explore it in detail.

The Mons

The first part of your vulva that you will see is the mons. The mons is a cushion of fat that sits over your pubic bone and is covered with hair. The skin covering your mons contains many nerves. Touching, licking, and stroking this area can be quite pleasurable.

The Outer Lips (Labia majora)

As you continue down your vulva, the next part that you will see are the outer lips. The outer lips are covered with hair on the outside. The inner surface is smooth, moist, and hairless. When you become excited, your labia swell and may feel full and tingly.

The Inner Lips (Labia minora)

Spread apart your outer lips, and you will see another set of smooth moist folds, the inner lips. These lips are filled with blood vessels and spongy tissue. They are covered with many nerve endings and are exquisitely sensitive. In fact, in some women, the inner lips are more sensitive—and provide more pleasure—than the clitoris. When you are sexually aroused, the labia fill with blood and become larger.

More than any other body part, the labia minora vary from one woman to the next. The color may range from pink to black, they may be small or large enough to protrude outside the labia majora, and they may be smooth or wrinkled. One labia may be longer or larger than the other. The labia drape over the head of the clitoris, forming the hood, and meet underneath the clitoris to form the *frenulum*. The area where the frenulum meets the head of the clitoris is the most sensitive area of the vulva for most women. This exquisite area responds best to light, gentle stimulation.

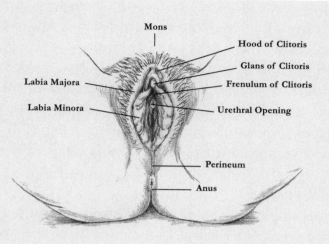

Mons

Hood of Clitoris

Glans of Clitoris

Labia Majora

Frenulum of Clitoris

Labia Minora

Urethral Opening

Perineum

Anus

The Vulva

The Clitoris

Pull back the hood formed by the labia minora and you will see a pea-shaped mass. That's the *glans,* or head, of your clitoris. But it doesn't end there; it continues toward your pubic bone as the *shaft* of the clitoris, then divides into two legs, or *crura,* that follow and attach to the pubic arch. The clitoris continues as the *vestibular bulbs,* two masses of erectile tissue between the labia minora and the crura. The bulbs partially surround the urethra and vagina, forming a powerful, sensitive clitoral-urethral-vaginal complex. During sexual stimulation, the bulbs fill with blood, making the opening to your vagina smaller and increasing your pleasure.

The size of the clitoris varies from one woman to another. But size doesn't matter. Even the smallest clitoris is capable of providing intense pleasure. The clitoris contains many nerve endings that make it very sensitive. For most women it is the most sensitive sexual body part. Some women, however, have few nerve endings on their clitoris and receive little, if any, pleasure when the clitoris is stimulated.

For those women, the labia minora, or another part of their sexual anatomy, holds the key to their pleasure. Knowing where your seat of sexual pleasure lies is key to sexual satisfaction.

When you become aroused, your clitoris fills with blood and becomes larger and stiffens. The sensitivity increases, and some women will notice a tingling, buzzing, or throbbing sensation. (By the way, your clitoris becomes filled with blood and erect during REM sleep in the same way that men have spontaneous erections while sleeping.)

The Urethra

The opening to the urethra is the small dimple that you see just below the clitoris. It is a short tube that carries urine from your bladder. It is surrounded by spongy erectile tissue and numerous small glands. The *female prostate gland* is the female equivalent of the male prostate gland and may be quite sensitive to sexual stimulation.

The Vagina

Below the urethra, you will see the opening to your vagina. Though we often think of it as only a hole down there, your vagina is a complex, amazing, and dynamic organ. The vagina is not actually a hole

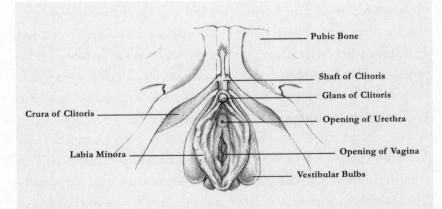

The Clitoris

but a potential space measuring between 3 and 6 inches in length. The surface of the vagina is warm and moist. It is surrounded by muscles and elastic tissue that enable it to stretch, and by blood vessels that swell when you become aroused, sending lubricating fluid into your vagina.

The vagina is a fascinating organ that is constantly changing, contracting, lubricating, and even cleansing itself. It contains many nerve endings and is quite sensitive. The opening to the vagina, the lower third, and the anterior (or front) wall tend to be the most sensitive areas of the vagina. Some women may find that their trigger spots are located on the back wall, or the top of the vagina near the cervix. You may have more sensitivity on one side of your vagina than others; changing the angle of insertion and thrusting during intercourse or manual sex play may give you tremendous pleasure, so be sure to experiment and see what feels good.

Through the front wall of the vagina is an area that is especially sensitive to stimulation in some women. A name for this area, the *G-spot,* was coined by Drs. Beverly Whipple and John Perry after the gynecologist, Dr. Ernst Grafenberg, who first described it. This area is located midway between the opening to the vagina and the cervix. When stimulated, this bean-sized area swells and may lead to orgasm.

The Perineum

Just below your vagina and before your anus is the perineum. The skin overlying this area contains many nerve endings. Stroking, pressing, licking, and massaging this area may bring much pleasure.

The Anus

Continue past the perineum and you reach the opening to the anus. The skin surrounding the anus contains many nerve endings and is very sensitive to touch. Beyond that opening is the anus, a tube that is 1½ inches long and sensitive to touch and stretch.

The Internal Sex Organs

The Cervix

If you insert your finger into your vagina as far as it can go, you will feel a structure that feels like the tip of your nose. That is your cervix, the lower part of your uterus. For some women, stimulation of the cervix provides pleasure and, sometimes, orgasm.

The Uterus

The uterus is a muscular organ that sits in the center of your pelvis. The lining of your uterus sheds every month, producing your menstrual period. It is also here that the baby implants when you become pregnant. The uterus contracts when you have an orgasm and, for some women, intensifies the pleasure.

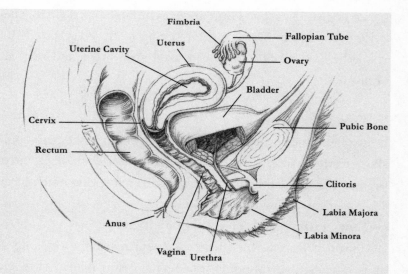

Female Internal Anatomy

The Fallopian Tubes

Extending from either side of your uterus are the fallopian tubes, which carry sperm and eggs to allow fertilization to take place.

The Ovaries

The ovaries are attached to the uterus by ligaments. Your ovaries release eggs every month and produce the hormones estrogen, progesterone, and testosterone.

The Pelvic Floor Muscles

The pelvic floor muscles are a group of muscles that form a hammock across the base of your pelvis and support your bladder, uterus, vagina, and rectum. One of these muscles, the pubococcygeal (or PC) muscle, stretches from your pubic bone to your tailbone. It surrounds your vagina and rectum like a sling. Often called the "love muscle," the PC is responsible for many of the pleasurable sensations that we feel during sex.

Other Pleasure Zones

The Breasts

Eighty percent of the female breast is composed of fat and connective tissue. The remainder is made of glands that produce milk and ducts that transport milk. The most sensitive part of the breast is the nipple and the surrounding areola and skin. When you are aroused, blood flow to your breasts increases, and your nipples become hard, erect, and sensitive. Stimulation of the breasts, particularly the nipples, can bring tremendous pleasure.

Dr. Hil Says: Every Woman Is Beautiful

Am I normal down there? is one of the most common questions that I hear from women. And it is easy to understand why. Unlike men, we cannot peer across to the person standing next to us at the urinal to discover whether we measure up. Nor are we likely to peep under the door of the toilet stall to compare and contrast what we possess with the woman next door. The typical woman's health book contains pictures that look nothing like real living women. So many of us are left feeling insecure and worried that what we see between our legs is unattractive and abnormal.

A recent study in the *British Journal of Obstetrics and Gynecology* reported the obvious: there is *no normal* when it comes to female genitals. Women vary widely in the size, color, shape, and texture of their labia, clitoris, and vagina. Yet there are physicians who play on the insecurities of women and offer unnecessary, expensive surgical alterations of their genitals. These procedures, called *vaginal rejuvenation,* claim to make female genitals look attractive and to improve women's sex lives. Other doctors offer to alter your G-spot, called *G-spot amplification* or the *G-Shot,* by injecting it with collagen, making it larger and more sensitive, again to improve your sex life.

After twenty-five years as a gynecologist, I can assure you that every woman is different. Each is unique, perfect, and beautiful. Surgery to change your natural feminine anatomy will not improve your sex life. In fact, there is a good possibility that it

continued

will make you feel much worse. Instead, celebrate and honor your unique feminine form. Only after you learn to love yourself will you be able to achieve the ultimate in sexual pleasure.

Skin

Any body part that is covered with skin has the potential to be a pleasure zone. Your skin is covered with nerves that respond to touching, stroking, massaging, sucking, and kissing.

Buttocks

These strong, erotic muscles are richly supplied with nerves that respond to stroking, squeezing, and massaging. The area at the base of your spine, where your buttocks begin, and the crease where your buttocks meet your upper thighs are particularly sensitive.

An Invitation to Explore

The point of this "anatomy lesson" is to encourage you to become familiar with your body, inside and out. Remember, if you don't know what's where—and, more important, what feels good—you won't be able to convey this essential information to your partner. Knowing your own body is the first step to pleasure.

3

. . . . .

His Body: Male Sexual Anatomy

When it comes to male sexual anatomy, there is so much more than meets the eye. If you want to help your partner achieve his maximal sexual potential and give you the kind of pleasure you desire and deserve, you need to learn how this not-so-simple creature's body really works.

External Anatomy

The Penis

When we think of male anatomy, what's the first thing that comes to your mind and his? Yes, the penis. At first glance, a man's penis appears to be no more than a tube nestled between his legs. We're familiar with the head, or glans; the body, or shaft; and the testicles tucked behind it.

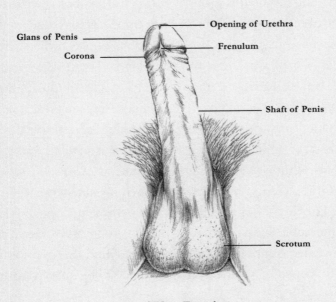

Glans of Penis

Corona

Opening of Urethra

Frenulum

Shaft of Penis

Scrotum

The Penis

That's the stuff you see. But the penis also has a bulb, or root, and two legs, or *crura*—important parts that you'll want to be familiar with. (By the way, I'm going to use the medical terms for all of his body parts because I want you to know what they are. You aren't expected to use them when you're whispering sweet nothings in his ear!)

The body of the penis is actually made up of three tubes, cylinders of spongy tissue full of blood vessels and nerves, each cylinder enveloped with a tough, fibrous layer. Two of the cylinders, the *corpora cavernosa*, lie side by side on the front of the penis. These tubes end at the bottom of the penis with two legs, the *crura*, which attach along the pubic bone. Don't ignore the crura; they contain many nerve endings that make them sensitive to touch. You can stimulate them by massaging the area along either side of the penis and scrotum.

The third spongy cylinder, the *corpus spongiosum*, lies on the back or underside of the penis in the groove between the two corpora cavernosa. The top of this cylinder forms the head of the penis; the bottom forms the bulb. Pay close attention to the head, the rim around the head (the *corona*), and the groove between the shaft and the corona (the *sulcus*). These areas are covered with nerve endings, so they're very sensitive—a good place to explore and experiment. The right touch there will give him immense satisfaction. Ask your man what kinds of licking, sucking, or stroking he finds pleasurable.

In the back or underside of the head, where it attaches to the shaft of the penis, is the *frenulum,* a band of tissue as exquisitely sensitive as your clitoris. Gently mouthing or touching him there will drive him nuts. The tiny slit on the head of the penis is the opening to the urethra, the tube encased in the corpus spongiosum that carries urine and semen out of the body. Some men find that gentle stimulation of this opening with a woman's tongue to be quite pleasurable as well.

The two corpora cavernosa and the corpus spongiosum are all wrapped in another layer of tough tissue and covered with thin, sensitive, hairless skin. The skin of the penis is so thin, in fact, that it can be damaged from the friction of vigorous intercourse if your vagina is dry. And it's loose so that it can accommodate the increase in size of the penis during an erection, and so that it can move freely during intercourse. If your guy is uncircumcised, the foreskin of his penis will cover the head but will pull back away from it when he is erect.

The Scrotum

The dark, hairy sac behind the penis is the scrotum, which houses and protects the two testes. You'll notice a line, or seam, down the middle of the scrotum. This *scrotal raphe* is sensitive in some men; touch and stroke this area to see if it brings him pleasure.

The Perineum

The perineum is the area between the base of the penis and the anus. The bulb of the penis is in this area, deeper inside the body;

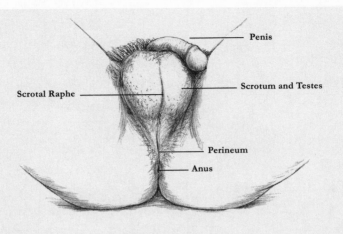

Penis

Scrotum and Testes

Scrotal Raphe

Perineum

Anus

The Perineum

deeper still is the prostate gland. The perineum also has a line down the center, the *perineal raphe,* which is highly sensitive in some men. Try gently stroking or massaging this area to see if it creates a pleasurable sensation for your partner.

Internal Anatomy

The Testes

Nestled inside the scrotum, as I mentioned, lie the two testes, or testicles, the smooth, oval-shaped organs that produce the hormone testosterone and the millions of sperm your man makes each day. The testes are exquisitely sensitive and must be handled gently, if at all. Some men like to have their testes sucked or fondled; others find manipulation of their testes uncomfortable. It's best to ask your man before you reach out and touch.

Your man's insides also include the *epididymis,* a tube that attaches to the surface of each testicle and stores sperm; the *vas deferens,* another tube that transports sperm from the epididymis to the urethra,

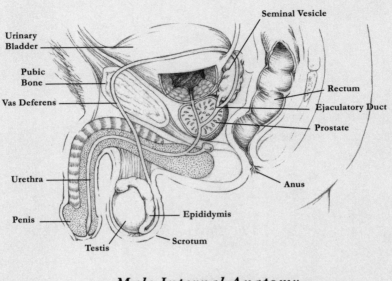

Male Internal Anatomy

where it's released during ejaculation; and the *seminal vesicles,* small glands that sit behind the prostate and are responsible for the secretions that make up most of a man's semen.

The Prostate

The prostate is a chestnut-sized organ that sits in front of the rectum, just below the bladder, and surrounds part of the urethra. It's responsible for making about a third of the seminal secretions. (The white fluid it creates helps the sperm survive in the vagina.) And it's so extremely sensitive that it's sometimes called the male G-spot. Massaging the prostate, through the perineum or rectum, can be very pleasurable for some men.

Breasts

The male breast is essentially just the nipple and surrounding areola. Men don't have the fat and glands that women have—the tissue that gives us our cup size—but, like ours, his nipples can be very sensitive and can become more sensitive when he's aroused. Interestingly, a few men can even experience orgasm through nipple stimulation alone.

What Happens During an Erection?

When a man becomes aroused, small glands called *Cowper's glands* begin to secrete a clear, slippery liquid. As this liquid exits the urethra, some men—not all—may actually become "wet," the way you do when you're aroused. As a man becomes more excited, arteries in the penis get wider, allowing blood flow to increase and fill spaces in the spongelike cylinders. At the same time, less blood is leaving through the veins, so all that extra blood flow causes the penis to start getting bigger and firmer. As the cylinders fill, they press against the fibrous covering, increasing pressure, until he's got a nice, hard erection. (You might also notice that the testes increase in size as they fill with blood. When your man is about to ejaculate, the scrotum pulls the testes up closer to the body.)

As your man becomes erect, the nerve endings that cover his penis ensure that it's more sensitive and responsive to pleasure, so just about anywhere you touch him is going to feel wonderful to him.

If you press on the perineum—the area between the anus and the scrotum—when he's erect, you'll feel the bulb of the penis; another sensitive area. Massaging him there will feel great to him.

Prostate Problems

Enlarged Prostate, Benign Prostatic Hyperplasia (BPH)

As men age, it is normal for the prostate gland to enlarge. Most men, at some point, will develop an enlarged prostate. When the prostate reaches a critical size, it may cause problems with urination and sexual dysfunction. Men may begin to have difficulty becoming erect or have problems with ejaculation. For some men with BPH, orgasm loses some of its intensity and pleasure.

Prostate Cancer

The second most common type of cancer among men (after skin cancer) is prostate cancer. The disease offers no specific signs or symptoms (an enlarged prostate doesn't lead to cancer) so the diagnosis may not be easy to make. Therefore, men aged fifty and older and those over the age of forty who are in high-risk groups (African-American men and those with a family history of prostate cancer) should have a prostate-specific antigen (PSA) blood test and digital rectal exam by their doctor once a year.

Prostate cancers can be fast or slow progressing, and there are several treatment options, including surgery and radiation therapy. Some men's ability to have an erection is affected by the treatment, so it can have an impact on your sexual life.

Healthy men will experience erections several times a night as they sleep. An erection, however, doesn't mean that he's dreaming of sex or is aroused. Most men will also experience an erection in the morning as they awake—again, not related to any particular sexual interest. Think of it as his body's way of practicing. However, that doesn't mean the two of you can't take advantage of a perfectly good erection. And if he's not aroused, it probably won't take much urging from you to get him there.

Ejaculation and Orgasm

Though we often use the terms interchangeably, it may surprise you to know that for men, ejaculation is not the same thing as orgasm.

Ejaculation occurs when the semen is forced out of his urethra. As sexual stimulation and sexual tension increase and reach a peak, the epididymis, vas deferens, seminal vesicles, and prostate gland begin to contract, pushing semen through the ejaculatory ducts and into the urethra. (At this point, he gets the pleasurable feeling that ejaculation is inevitable and can't be stopped.) As the semen enters the urethra, the muscle around the root of the penis and pelvic floor muscles begin to contract every eight-tenths of a second, forcing semen out of the urethra.

In young men, semen may be propelled several inches or even more than a foot. As a man ages, semen may only dribble out. Either way, he only releases about a teaspoon of the thick fluid, though it may seem like more, and either way, his ejaculation is intensely pleasurable. After ejaculation, a man enters a period during which he can't produce an erection and orgasm is impossible. This refractory period may be as short as a few minutes or as long as a few days.

That's an ejaculation. An orgasm is that peak pleasurable sensory experience that occurs those seconds *just before* he ejaculates, when he feels the inevitability of the ejaculation. Some men have perfected methods that allow them to experience orgasm—even multiple orgasms—without ejaculation.

The key is to deliberately stop ejaculation at that point just before it becomes inevitable. (Right before the "I'm coming" moment.) A man may stop thrusting for a few seconds in order to hold off the inevitable release. Or, if he's developed a very disciplined mind, he can divert his attention from the sensation in his penis. (If, at this point, he directs his attention to his pelvic movements instead of the thrusting of his penis, he can find a way to make more contact with your clitoris, increasing the pleasurable experience for you.) Either way, he has held himself at that peak moment awhile longer and can bring himself to that moment again. That means waves of pleasure for him during your lovemaking session. When he does ejaculate, it's very intense and satisfying.

Here's where wearing a condom can help. It ever so slightly lessens the intensity of feeling in his penis, allowing him more control over when he comes to climax.

Changes in the Aging Male

The average guy reaches his sexual peak in his late teens: He wants sex and can perform just about all the time. As a man ages, his sexual capacity will change. The natural decrease in testosterone that occurs as a man ages will leave some men with less desire for sex; he'll want it less often. Another man will still want sex, but it may take longer for him to achieve an erection, and sometimes he won't have one at all. He may feel intensely aroused, in fact, but his penis may be slow to respond. Whereas just the idea of sex or seeing something (or someone) he finds sexy once made him rise to attention, now it's a pleasant thought in his mind that may not have as immediate an impact on his penis. That doesn't mean an older man can't ever have an erection or enjoy great sex. It just means you'll have to do more work—or should we say "play"—to get him there.

The aging penis is fragile and sensitive; it not only needs more time to respond, but usually needs direct contact to become hard. You can help his erection along by stroking his penis with your hands or suckling him with your mouth. When you're fondling him, realize that the shaft and head of an older man's penis may be less sensitive than those of a younger man, and he may need a stronger touch. You may have to give him persistent, prolonged stimulation to bring him to climax.

Even if you're using your best foreplay techniques, your older man may not get rock hard. Whereas his penis once pointed up when erect, it may point straight out or even down a bit. Don't worry; this is normal. The position of the penis doesn't inhibit his ability to feel intense pleasure or to give it. And the fact that it may take him longer to experience orgasm is good news for you if you like long love-making sessions; you'll have plenty of time to enjoy the ride.

Be aware that your partner may lose the sense of excited anticipation that comes when ejaculation is imminent, and the orgasm may be less intense. He'll likely release a smaller amount of semen—in a dribble rather than a strong squirt—and the refractory period—the amount of time until he's able to have another orgasm—is generally longer than when he was younger. It may last up to twenty-four hours.

None of this is necessarily bad news for you. His need for extra attention may mean he'll want to return the favor. Many women find older men to be more patient, loving, affectionate, and concerned with the pleasure of their partner. And while they may not be able to perform two or three times in a night, some men find that they receive as much, if not more, pleasure from other kinds of physical intimacy—hugging, snuggling, spooning—than from intercourse. What woman would argue with that? All these are reasons some women feel that the older man is the best lover.

My advice to women with older partners is to embrace the change and enjoy the process. Be patient, be understanding, don't pressure him to perform, and don't focus so much on that erection. Consider it a bonus. Besides, there's plenty of lovemaking that can happen with or without it and plenty of pleasure to be had for both of you.

II

. . . . .

Getting the Sex You Want

4
. . . . .

Bold and Beautiful: Gaining Sexual Confidence

We've all seen her, a woman whose face and body would never grace the cover of a fashion magazine, yet all eyes follow her when she enters the room. She walks with a certain flair, exudes confidence, and positively radiates sexual energy. Everything about her says "I am hot, I am desirable, I am sexy—and I know it." She is a woman who feels comfortable in her own skin and confident with her sexuality, and that self-assurance is contagious. Everyone—men, women, and babies—want to be around her and her positive attitude. Her positive attitude makes everyone around her feel as good as she does. Have you ever wanted to be that woman?

Ask a group of men what they find most attractive about a woman and chances are they will mention *confidence*. A woman who feels attractive, comfortable with her body and sexuality, will naturally appear sexier to others. It is not necessary to look like a supermodel. And you should not allow beauty to be defined by men or the media. Create your own definition of beauty, and you are the star.

When you feel sexually confident you take responsibility for your own pleasure. You are able to relax, let go of your inhibitions, and fully enjoy sex. You know what you want and how to get it. You feel comfortable initiating sex and have no qualms about letting your partner know your needs and desires.

The key to becoming sexually confident is to love yourself and truly believe that you are deserving of pleasure. Every woman, even the meekest among us, can learn to embrace her inner vixen. All it takes is a change in attitude. Don't *ask* if you are sexy; *know* that you are. Then do something every day to remind yourself just how wonderful you are. If you need help getting started, below are a few suggestions to help you on your way. Think of it like exercising: The more often you do it the stronger and more confident you will become.

Steps to Becoming a Sexually Confident Woman

- Self-pleasure regularly. It helps you understand your body parts and how they work. We will explore this idea more in the next chapter.
- Dress sexy every day. Why wait for a special occasion to feel special? Throw out the faded baggy sweatpants. In fact, get rid of any clothes that make you feel old, fat, or unattractive. Don't even wear them around the house when no one is looking.

    Dress every day just because it makes you feel good about you. Work hard to feel attractive for yourself, not for him. For him, it becomes a chore; for your self, it becomes a necessity! It gives you the desire to walk tall, put a swing in your step, because you know that you look marvelous! Dress in colors that compliment your complexion. Wear sensual fabrics that feel good against your skin.

✎ Invest in sexy underwear. Walk into any Victoria's Secret or Frederick's of Hollywood, and you can almost feel the sexual heat in the air. Few things make a woman feel sexier than a pretty matching bra and panty or thong set. Wear it under your everyday clothing. Yes, even on days when only you will see it. Your sexy secret will increase your sexual thoughts and your desire. And if you feel like sharing this bit of personal information with someone else, feel free.

✎ Rid yourself of negative sexual messages and replace them with positive, empowering messages. If you received negative messages about sex as a child, write them down and change them into positive ones. Seek professional therapy for events in your past that might have caused you to feel ashamed or repressed about sex.

Discard all negativity. Does that magazine make you feel inadequate? Don't read it. Is that television show less than woman-positive? Don't watch it. Does your partner make negative comments about you and make you feel less than beautiful? Get rid of him. Life is too short.

✎ Adopt a positive attitude about life. All things are possible. There are no limits to what you can do.

✎ Keep a journal. Complete this sentence: "*One thing I love about me is____*" and write down your thoughts and feelings daily.

✎ Look in the mirror every day and repeat the following affirmation:

I am a sexy, sensual woman. I deserve sexual pleasure. I, and I alone, own my sexuality. I know how to bring pleasure to myself and to my partner. I love my body.

✎ When you're alone, walk around your home naked. As you pass mirrors, glance and appreciate the beauty of your body. Note the smooth curves of the feminine form. Now, practice your "Lola" walk: head is high, back straight, shoulders back, chest out, while your hips sway gently from side to side. The movement is subtle but unmistakably sexy. (When I was growing up in Alabama, we used to call it "switching.")

If you have a private backyard, take your nudity experience outside. Savor the feel of the sun against your skin. Twirl in the wind with arms outstretched. Breathe deeply. Take a flower or leaf and gently brush it along the surface of your skin. Feel alive. Focus on the pleasure.

✎ Get a makeover, including hair, manicure, pedicure, makeup. For maintenance, treat yourself to one of these treats regularly (at least twice a month).

✎ Write an erotic story in which you are the main character.

✎ Initiate sex. Tonight.

✎ Study sex manuals and be willing to experiment and try new techniques.

✎ Begin an exercise program and work out at least three times a week. A sexy, toned body will give you the confidence to make love in any position . . . with the lights on. More about this a bit later.

✎ Smile. Nothing shows confidence more than a sexy "come-hither" smile.

✎ Create a romantic atmosphere in your home.

Den of Desire:
The Feng Shui of Pleasure

To boost your confidence, create surroundings that make you feel good, sensual, and put you in the mood for sex. No, you may not want your bedroom to look like a bordello. (Then again, maybe a dimly lit room with a big mahogany bed, fringed velvet drapery, and rich satin sheets is just the thing for you.) Whatever your personal style, your surroundings should make you feel comfortable, relaxed, and uninhibited.

Below are some personal strategies based on the ancient art of feng shui that you can use to help energize your bedroom and transform it into your own dazzling den of desire. I call my version "*fun* shui."

Clear out the clutter. A cluttered bedroom results in low, slow energy, since positive energy can't move freely through a crowded, messy space. You can give your sex life a needed boost by cleaning house—literally!

Seek out sex symbols. Decorate with items that symbolize, *for you,* passion and intimacy. Hang artwork showing lovers. Use red, pink, or white accessories and linens. Place a vase of fragrant fresh flowers by the bed. Put two pink or red candles side by side somewhere in the room. (If you're looking to attract a mate, always decorate with pairs of objects and pictures showing two people.)

continued

Provide a passageway for love. Make sure the door to your bedroom opens easily and completely. You want to let love in! Allow the free flow of romantic energy to enter your space.

Make room for sex and romance. If you want a new relationship, you have to make room for another person in your home even if you don't know who that person is yet. Once you've made room for that special someone, visualize the person who might be your match.

Douse old flames. Making room for a new love might also mean stomping out the memories of an old flame. Don't hold on to anything that reminds you of failed past relationships; dump any old love letters, clothes, or pictures that have bad memories attached to them.

Reposition your bed. Center your bed so that there is equal space on either side. This will help you and your partner share equal power and enjoyment in the relationship. Ideally, try to position your bed on the opposite wall from the door but not directly in line with it.

Use color carefully. When it comes to the colors you use in your bedroom, some are "sexier" than others. Blue is cool and keeps appetites in check—not something you want in your bedroom. White is too sterile, and yellow is too intellectual. Lavender encourages chastity, so keep that in mind for your teenager's bedroom but not for yours. What's left? Paint your

continued

walls the color of rose quartz or a tropical sunset to cast a warm glow on your skin.

Ditch the distractions. Get your computer, dirty laundry, television, bills, or exercise equipment out of the bedroom. Ban from your bedroom anything that doesn't promote romance, relationships, or sex or that might distract your attention from your relationship.

5
. . . . .

Knowing Yourself: Discovering What Feels Good

Ultimate sexual pleasure begins with self-discovery. Becoming familiar with your personal pleasure centers and where and how you like to be touched is the key to achieving sexual satisfaction. I encourage women to take the time to physically get in touch with their bodies, to look at and touch themselves all over. It really is the only way you'll be able to discover and describe the kind of pleasure you long for. It's a journey well worth taking!

The First Step

Sexual pleasure is not only physical, but emotional as well. That's why great sex can bring you to tears and make you feel emotionally closer to your partner. Quite often we women are so tuned in to, and caught up with the needs of, our partners and other family members that we forget to consider what *we* like.

One day I was completing a relationship survey in a popular magazine. It was relaxing and I was happily reassured that I could easily answer all of the questions. I knew exactly what my husband's favorite color was, his favorite book, even his favorite brand of boxers. My euphoria was short-lived, however, when I realized that I could not answer these questions for myself. What was *my* favorite color, book, or brand of underwear? Answers that came so quickly earlier were no longer automatic. When was the last time that I spent any time thinking about myself—what I liked and what made me truly happy? It was a life-altering moment.

Before you can begin to discover what feels good physically, you need to take steps to get more in touch with your emotional side. To achieve the rich, satisfying sex that you want, need, and deserve, you must take a journey of self-awareness. Here are some exercises that will help you on your way.

 ❧ Take a mini retreat alone. It can be as short as half a day or as long as several days. Choose a location where you can be totally alone: a secluded bench in a quiet arboretum, a deserted beach, or a hotel room are all options. Use the time to answer a list of questions about yourself. What is your favorite color? Comfort food? Book? Movie? Song? Season? Time of day? What is your favorite part of your body and why? What makes you laugh? What location do you feel most at ease in? Who is your best friend and why? If you could do anything that you wanted right now, what would it be? What is your favorite way to spend an evening? If you could have only one possession, what would it be? What gives you the greatest pleasure? What is your passion? Add your own questions to this list and write the answers down in a journal.

- Go to your favorite restaurant alone. Sit quietly (no books allowed). While eating food that gives you pleasure, concentrate on the taste, texture, temperature, and the tingling sensations of your taste buds. Savor the pleasure.

- Take fifteen minutes and write a list of things that make you happy. Don't waste time thinking about whether your response is a good one or what others will think if they see the list. Write as many as you can in the fifteen minutes and then stop.

- With a blank canvas and acrylic paints, paint your emotions. Don't spend time trying to be an artist, just go with your feelings.

- Spend an evening alone doing whatever you want, whatever makes you happy. Pretend that you are the only person in the world. Watch your favorite movies (the ones he never wants to watch with you), read your favorite books, eat your favorite foods (and calories be damned!), listen to your favorite music, smile, laugh, cry, or just *be*.

- Think of your five senses: sight, sound, taste, touch, and smell. Make a list of ways you receive pleasure through each of your senses. For example: *The sound of rushing waves of the ocean gives me pleasure.* Or: *The scent of his skin gives me pleasure.* Make a habit of stimulating each of those senses every day.

To achieve the best sex, you must know who you are, what you want, and what makes you happy on an emotional level. Only when you know what truly makes you tingle can you fully begin to accept pleasure into your life.

Solo Pleasure

Begin your journey by luxuriating in a warm bath. Take time to indulge all your senses. Fill your tub with warm water and sprinkle in some bath salts or scented oil. Light some aromatic candles, turn out the lights, and turn on some soft music. The goal is to make you feel pampered, sexy, and sensual.

After your bath, stand in front of a full-length mirror and take a good look at your body. Instead of focusing on what you don't like, or worrying about losing those last ten pounds, take a moment to marvel at every part of your body and appreciate their beauty: your luscious, moist lips and silky smooth skin; the sensual curves of your neck, butt, hips, thighs, breasts, or abdomen. Sway your hips from side to side, bump and grind, perform an erotic dance for your eyes only.

Learning to love and accept your body will make it easier for you to abandon yourself to sex, alone or with a partner. You can kick off the sheets, turn on the lights, and concentrate on pleasure.

Finding the Right Touch

Now that you've become comfortable with how your body looks, it is time to get in touch with how it feels. Lie down on a comfortable surface such as crisp, clean sheets or a warm blanket. Drizzle a few drops of warm, mildy scented massage oil on your hands and, slowly, begin by gently rubbing the oil on your neck. Revel in how it feels to have your hands glide across your slick skin. Work your way to your shoulders and down your arms. Caress your breasts and down to your abdomen. Stroke your lower back and butt, then move down to your thighs, calves, and feet. Explore every inch of your body.

Spend a few minutes stroking and massaging your breasts. Using the tip of one finger, gently circle each nipple. Gently squeeze them

between your index finger and thumb and pull slightly. You may notice that your nipple becomes firm and erect. Take your sweet time
to work your way down your body. If you rush, you won't learn to
appreciate the feel of your skin, the warmth of your flesh. As you
stroke your body, take note of any extrasensitive spots and the type
of touch that elicits the most pleasure. Try different types of strokes,
pressures, and speeds. Concentrate on the pleasurable sensations.

Next, sit in front of the mirror or use a handheld mirror to take a
good look at your genitals. Touch each part, saying the name of each
out loud. You can use medical terms like *labia* and *clitoris* or other
terms like *lips* and *clit,* whichever make you feel more comfortable.
Observe the complexity, color, texture, shape, scent, moisture, and
beauty of your vulva and the opening of your vagina. Take your time.
Relax. Become comfortable with your unique natural taste and scent.

Lie on your back, side, or stomach, whichever is most comfortable for you. Use your fingers to apply a generous amount of water-
based lubricant, such as Astroglide or KY Liquid, to your vulva and
the opening to your vagina. Breathe slowly and concentrate on the
sensations. Now slowly slide the fingers of one hand from your mons
to the opening of your vagina and back. Start slowly, then gradually
pick up the speed. Use one or two fingers to lightly stroke your inner
lips, up and down and then in circles. Slide your hands up and over
the hood of your clitoris. Rub each side of your clitoris, then along
its length. Make circular motions to include inner lips, clitoris, and
opening to your vagina. Vary the intensity, pressure, direction, and
speed of your strokes. Breathe deeply and focus your attention on
the skin beneath your fingertips. Make a mental note of how your
body responds to your fingers: which areas tingle at your touch and
which give you the most pleasure. These are the places you'll want to
explore further, by yourself and with your partner.

Insert one or two fingers into your vagina again. Be aware of the
moisture and warmth as you move your finger along all of the walls
of your vagina. Explore the opening, the sides, the front and back.

Reach up toward the top of your vagina and touch your cervix—it feels somewhat like the tip of your nose—then circle it with the tip of your finger. Reach farther into your vagina to its very top. Press here and remain still for a few seconds. Relax and breathe. Press the back and then the front walls of your vagina.

If you are interested, you can try a G-spot massage. It may be difficult to reach your G-spot at first, but with a little ingenuity, you can successfully stroke this sensitive spot. Try lying on your back and bringing your knees in toward your chest. (Alternatively, lie on your stomach and raise your hips slightly.) Insert your middle finger, index finger, or both deeply into your vagina. As you withdraw your finger, press against the front of your vagina and urethra and curl your finger in a beckoning gesture. You may initially have the sensation that you need to urinate. This is normal and may soon be replaced by a warm, pleasurable sensation. Note that it may take several sessions before you begin to feel pleasure. Some women never find stimulation of this area to be pleasurable. Through experimentation and exploration, you may discover that your sensitive spot lies elsewhere in your vagina.

Pleasure is discovering what makes you feel good and indulging without guilt or shame.

Treat Yourself as You Would Treat a Lover

Make a date with yourself. Prepare as if you are getting ready for a night of erotic pleasure with your lover. The key to this exercise is to treat yourself the way you would treat a treasured lover and the way you would like your lover to treat you. If you would begin the perfect date with a gourmet meal, prepare one just for you. If it turns you on to hear that your body is beautiful, say it out loud. If you would end the date with mad passionate lovemaking, give yourself the most intense pleasurable experience possible.

Remember, exploring what feels good—on your own—is where pleasure begins. So take time out to explore, without judgment or pressure. What you learn in the course of your research will serve you well!

Working It Out: Improving Your Sexual Fitness

In addition to familiarizing yourself with your body's pleasure zones, you'll need to take good care of your body in order to maximize pleasure. In particular, you'll need to make exercise part of your daily routine. Why is exercise an aphrodisiac? First, physical fitness contributes to overall good health, enabling every part of your body to function better. Since sex is a total-body experience, your enjoyment increases when your muscles, nerves, heart, lungs, and blood vessels are at their peak performance. And when you're healthier and more toned, you have a better self-image and feel more attractive. Nothing is sexier than that kind of confidence.

Just for Sex

While any and all exercise can improve your sex life in general, I recommend a few exercises that are specific to your sexual health. These moves focus on the pelvic area, strengthening and toning the muscles around your genitals.

Kegel Exercises

You'll find mentions of Kegel exercises throughout this book. I swear by them because they're the very best thing you can do to strengthen the PC (pubococcygeal) muscle, the muscle running from your pubic bone to your tailbone. (Imagine a sling enclosing your vagina and rectum.) When your PC muscle is toned and strong, you can feel more and *do* more during sex. For example, you can grip your partner's penis tighter when he's inside you, or treat him to a squeeze-release, squeeze-release action that will drive him wild. Squeeze your PC muscle as he withdraws his penis during intercourse. When your muscle is strong, you may produce a "snapping" sound. You can increase your pleasure by moving his penis so that your most sensitive spots are stroked.

The easiest way to learn how to perform Kegels correctly is to wait until you're going to the bathroom: Sit on the toilet bowl with your legs spread apart as far as possible to make sure you use only the PC muscle. Begin to urinate, then squeeze your pelvic floor muscles to stop the flow of urine. You are using your PC muscle. Now practice squeezing and releasing, stopping and starting the urine flow until you have a good idea where your muscle is and how to tighten it. But you don't have to wait until you're in the bathroom to perform Kegels; because you're exercising an internal muscle, you can do Kegels anywhere, anytime, and no one will be the wiser.

Try to do two daily sessions of twenty-five to fifty repetitions each. Start with an empty bladder and hold each contraction, or squeeze, for as long as you can. At first, you may only be able to contract for a few seconds, but eventually you'll be able to hold it for ten seconds or more.

It may take months before you actually start enjoying the benefits of a stronger PC muscle. But if you establish a daily routine, you can expect to notice a difference in your sex life in a matter of weeks. Your vaginal sensations will be heightened for more pleasure, and you may experience stronger and longer lasting orgasms. Try it and see!

PC Weight Training

You can increase the strength of your love muscle (PC muscle) by adding weight training to your exercise routine.

A device called the *Kegelcisor* is a small metal barbell to exercise your PC muscle. Begin by warming your barbell under warm water, then lubricate well. Lie on your back with your knees bent. Slide the barbell into your vagina. Squeeze your PC muscle to move the bar. Start slowly and work up to fifty squeezes a day. You can order it from any adult-toy website.

Betty Dodson's Barbell is similar to the Kegelcisor. Squeeze and release your PC muscle as you slowly insert and then withdraw the barbell. You can order it from *www.bettydodson.com*.

Natural Contours Energie Kegel Exerciser is a sleek, smooth, ergonomically shaped barbell. Insert it into the vagina and squeeze your PC muscle to move the barbell. You can purchase it online at *www.natural-contours.com*.

Vaginal cones are tampon-shaped weights that help strengthen your PC muscle. They come in sets of four to five cones of increasing weight. Place the lightest cone into your vagina and squeeze your PC muscle to keep the weight from falling out. When you can walk for fifteen minutes while holding the weight inside, advance to the next weight size. You can obtain cones from your doctor's office or online at *www.aswechange.com*.

Kegel Exercises for Men

Men can benefit from Kegel exercises, too. If your man learns to contract the PC muscle just before his orgasm, he'll be able to delay ejaculation for an extended sexual encounter; and his orgasms will feel more intense. In addition, when his muscles are strong, he can move his penis in interesting ways during intercourse, increasing the chance that he will hit your most sensitive spots.

He can find his pelvic floor muscles using the same method you did: by stopping the flow of urine. He should inhale as he contracts, then exhale as he fully relaxes. He can start with just ten to twenty squeezes per session and work his way up as the muscle strengthens. Before you know it, both of you will gain better control over your sex organs for a more intense sexual encounter.

Pelvic Lifts

Pelvic lifts help you develop the muscles that enable you to arch your back, thrust your hips, and bring your pelvis into closer contact with his. Lie on your back with your knees bent and slightly apart. Put your feet flat on the floor and keep your arms at your sides. Inhale, tighten your abdominals and buttocks, and lift your pelvis toward the ceiling until your back is completely straight (don't arch). Breathe while you hold the position for a minimum of ten seconds. Then exhale as you lower your buttocks to the floor. Repeat.

The Butterfly

The butterfly will help increase your flexibility during sex. Lie on your back on a bed or a mat. Bend your knees and bring the soles of your feet together, letting your knees fall open. Pull your feet toward your body until they touch your behind. If you're doing it right, your knees will be facing opposite sides of the bed, much like the wings of a butterfly. Ideally, your heels will touch your buttocks, and your knees and legs will be flat against the bed. (But that's for the most flexible among us.) To start, just try to keep your heels as close to your butt as you can, and try lowering your knees toward the bed as much as possible without forcing them. The idea is to get a good stretch along your inner thighs and open up the pelvic area. Try holding the position for sixty seconds. Then slowly bring the knees back together and relax.

You can also do this exercise sitting up or sitting back-to-back with a partner.

Don't Forget Your Overall Fitness Level

While I recommend the above exercises to improve your sexual fitness, so that you can achieve maximum pleasure with your partner, I encourage all women (and men too!) to start and stick with a regular fitness routine, incorporating cardio and strength training. This is essential to good health, so that you can enjoy a long life and a pleasurable sex life. If you're not already doing so, start your fitness routine today.

7
. . . . .

Body Talk: Communicating Your Needs

Communicating with your partner about what brings you pleasure is vital to a good sexual relationship. Yet women often find it difficult to ask for what they need and desire. We fear hurting our partner's feelings, or worry that he will think we are "bad" or that we have had a secret sexual rendezvous. And all too commonly we assume that he should somehow "just know" how to bring us pleasure. You can't expect your partner to be a mind reader. *It's up to you to take responsibility for your own pleasure.*

So before we get to the pleasurable business of finding out what feels good for *you* in the chapters to come, I want to stress the importance of keeping the lines of communication open. After all, if you learn what really turns you on and you keep that precious knowledge to yourself, you'll miss out on finding pleasure with your partner, and that's something every woman deserves.

If you never tell him how he can make your toes curl, thighs quiver, and your juices flow, you run the risk of it never happening. Remaining silent will increase the chance that you will end up frustrated, resentful, and sexually unsatisfied. And these feelings will eventually get in the way of intimacy and negatively affect your relationship.

Telling your man what you'd like him to do doesn't mean putting together a presentation complete with diagrams. If you're the shy type who can't imagine putting your sexual desires into words, there are other ways to let him know how to rock your world.

Nonverbal communication can work wonders in this area. Use your body to tell him what feels good. For instance, you can place your hand over his and direct him to the right location, the right pressure, and the right speed to bring you pleasure. You might shift your hips or change positions to help him reach your hot spot. The noises you make during sex can also relay feelings of pleasure. Moans, sighs, giggles say to him, "I like what you are doing. Give me more!" One of the best nonverbal ways to relay information about how to bring you pleasure is to self-pleasure in front of your partner. There is simply no better way for him to learn what turns you on.

Verbal communication may be a bit more difficult. Talking about sex openly may make you feel more vulnerable than nonverbal communication does. Despite how awkward it might feel, some issues can be resolved only by talking with your partner. Telling your partner what you need and desire is the best and most direct way to ensure that you are both satisfied.

To keep the lines of communication open, check out the following list of tips on how to talk about sex with your partner.

- **Set aside time to talk.** This is a discussion to have when neither of you is rushed, distracted, or upset. Talk about it when things are good, and, more important, when things could be better, and be direct and honest in your discussion.

❣ **Know what you want.** Before you begin, make sure that you are aware of what brings you pleasure; it makes it easier to share your needs and desires with your partner. That way, you can provide him with positive suggestions instead of telling him what he does wrong.

❣ **Accentuate the positives.** Try to minimize the negatives. This isn't about criticizing or blaming him for what he doesn't do. Focus on what he does well, and suggest other things that he can do to satisfy you.

❣ **Speak in "I" terms.** Begin your statements with "I" rather than "you." That way you focus on your feelings rather than on what you perceive as his flaws. For instance, say "I would love to have more oral sex. You are so good at it," rather than "You never give me enough oral sex."

❣ **Make requests.** Make sexual *requests* rather than demands.

❣ **Meet him halfway.** Ask your partner what he likes and *listen* to his response. Ask him what you can do to make his sexual experience better. Opening the lines of communication for him will make it easier for him to reciprocate.

Dr. Hil says:

ASK FOR WHAT YOU WANT!

When and Where Should You Talk About Sex?

When is the best time to talk about sex? The answer is, "It depends." Some issues can, and should, be discussed in bed, before or after sex. Other issues are best discussed anywhere but in the bedroom, and at a time when you are both relaxed and open to communication. For more specific advice on how to broach the subject, consider the following scenarios:

You want to try something new.

You can start this conversation either in or out of bed. Be direct and simply make a request. If you are having difficulty getting started, a good way to begin is to read a sexy book or magazine article, watch an erotic video, or share a fantasy with your partner that includes the desired sexual technique. Then make a statement such as "I'd love to try that." Or you could just initiate sex, take charge, and, as the saying goes, just do it.

He wants sex, but you don't.

Each member of a couple should feel comfortable telling the other that they are not in the mood for sex. It is common for two people to be on different sexual wavelengths from time to time. If he wants one activity, like intercourse, and you don't, you might consider offering him an alternative, like oral sex. Alternatively, you might lovingly offer a rain date.

If you find that the two of you have totally conflicting sexual needs, you need to have this conversation outside the bedroom. Explain your desire level, listen to his, and work toward a compromise that fulfills both of your needs.

He does something during sex that causes you discomfort or pain.

If you are having pain, it's important to tell him as it is happening. You should not grit your teeth and bear it for fear of hurting his feelings or interfering with his pleasure. Sex should be mutually enjoyable. If it hurts, speak up and work with your partner to make sex a more enjoyable experience for both of you.

He does something wonderful, and you want more of it.

Any time is a good time to have *this* conversation. Chances are he will be thrilled to get the accolades. You can applaud during sex by making lots of approving sounds: moans, groans, sexy talk. After sex is a good time to review the wonderful moves and techniques that he introduced. He will love you for it, and it is more likely that he will remember it the next time. To increase his arousal in the future, whisper how much you enjoyed that particular experience in his ear.

He wants to try something new, but you don't feel comfortable with it.

Again, honesty is the best policy. You might tell him that you are not comfortable with that particular sexual technique right now. Then offer another option (preferably new and exciting) as a compromise. You want to make sure that you don't make him feel judged, abnormal, or hurt in any way, so be gentle but firm, and if possible offer an alternative he won't want to pass up.

He tries something new, but you're not thrilled with it.

Begin the conversation by pointing out something positive about his sexual techniques. Then be honest and direct in telling him that the new technique gives you less pleasure. End the conversation by reiterating what *does* turn you on (and then do it!).

You want more sex.

This conversation should take place outside the bedroom. Begin by telling him how much you love him and enjoy the intimacy that you share. Then tell him how you would love to have more. Listen to his response. Often he will be thinking the same thing. If that's not the case, work with him on a compromise that is acceptable to the two of you.

You want to talk about safer sex.

Conversations about safer sex should take place long before you get to the bedroom. You and your partner should talk about your past sexual histories. Condom use should be understood and negotiated before you become intimate. Waiting until you are in the throes of passion will make it difficult to make good decisions. (For more information, see the chapter on safer sex.)

Continuing the Conversation

Keep in mind that talking about pleasure isn't a one-time deal. Rather, as you explore what feels good—for each of you—you'll need to keep the lines of communication open, exploring the pleasurable possibilities, with conversations in and out of the bedroom.

III
. . . . .

Ultimate Sex

8
· · · · ·

The Pleasures of Cunnilingus

Good cunnilingus is like a priceless gift. When performed well, it provides most women with immense pleasure. In fact, it's the easiest way for most of us to experience orgasm. Yet myths and misconceptions about the female body have made some women, and men, reluctant to delve deeply into this practice.

If your partner shies away from cunnilingus, it is important to let him know how much you want to experience this form of oral pleasure. Allay any fears that he might have about hygiene, a common male concern, by offering to shower together prior to sex. If it is lack of experience that is causing him concern, agree to work with him to help develop his own unique cunnilingus style. Offer him one of the many sex guides that are devoted to the art of cunnilingus and read it together. There simply is no excuse for a man to refuse to provide you with oral pleasure. If he remains reluctant, feel free to refuse to perform fellatio until he changes his mind.

To fully enjoy the pleasure of cunnilingus, incorporate the following tips:

Check Your Attitude. How do you feel about the appearance, smell, and taste of your genitals? You are not alone if your answer is "Not good." Many of us are not comfortable with our most intimate parts. We have been conditioned since childhood to think of our genitals as ugly, smelly, and unclean. Having a man up close and personal to that part of your body may make you feel uncomfortable. You may worry that he, too, will find your female anatomy distasteful and be turned off by its appearance, scent, or taste. Your fears are unfounded. Most men are turned on by the sight of the female vulva and vagina, and the scent is a natural aphrodisiac.

To get in touch with your genitals, take a close look with the mirror. Appreciate the color, texture, moisture, and complexity of your most intimate parts. Become familiar with your unique scent. Place a clean finger in your vagina. Remove it, wave it several inches in front of your nose, and breathe deeply. This clean, natural scent is powerful and arousing. Now take that same finger, place it in your mouth, and taste your secretions. The flavor of your vaginal fluids may range from sweet to slightly salty or have no detectable taste at all. The taste may vary throughout the month and be affected by what you eat, drink, or smoke. Smoking, alcohol, recreational drugs, medications, vitamins, coffee, and foods like onion, garlic, asparagus, and curry may give you a less than pleasant taste. Eating lots of fresh fruits and vegetables and drinking lots of water will help to keep your unique flavor pleasant and fresh.

Learn to receive pleasure. Women are givers. And sometimes it is the most difficult thing in the world for us to receive pleasure. In order to reach the heights of sexual pleasure, you must be able to be selfish and concentrate only on your own pleasure. Cunnilingus is the perfect opportunity to lie back, forget your worries, and be pleasured by your mate. His pleasure is dependent on your pleasure. Few things will make your partner happier than being able to give you the ultimate sexual experience. *Orgasm should not be a goal,* so there is no need to worry about how long it will take you to reach it. So relax, breathe, and concentrate only on the pleasure that you are receiving. Give yourself permission to receive pleasure. You deserve it.

Take care of hygiene. You may feel more relaxed and less concerned about your scent if you shower or bathe before receiving oral sex. There is no need to douche or use deodorant sprays and perfumes. In fact, these products may increase your risk of infections and cause allergic reactions in your mate. Use only a mild cleansing bar and water, and dry well. If your pubic hair is very long and wild, trim it a bit with barber shears to give him easier access. Then comb to remove stray hairs. Some women find that shaving or waxing some or all of the pubic hair increases the sensitivity and pleasure of cunnilingus.

Choose a good position. Find a position that is comfortable for you and your partner. You need to feel relaxed in order to enjoy the sensations. The best position is one in which you lie on your back with your knees bent. He lies between your legs. This position gives his tongue and mouth the best access to the most sensitive part of your clitoris and vagina. You can increase access to your vagina and buttocks by propping your buttocks on pillows.

The 69 position is exotic and preferred by some men. This position, however, makes it difficult for you to concentrate on your pleasure while providing pleasure to your partner. As women, it is more likely that we will focus on providing oral pleasure to our mate and ignore the pursuit of our own pleasure. In addition, the position of his tongue makes it difficult to reach the most sensitive part of the clitoris.

Sitting on his face, well, actually kneeling over his face, is another option. The position of his tongue is good, as is access to your vagina.

His hands are free to roam and increase your pleasure. For some women, this position is psychologically stimulating and provides a feeling of power or domination. It creates tension in your thighs, however, and you may feel that it is difficult to fully relax.

You can also sit in a chair or on the edge of a table, while he kneels in front of you. Be sure to provide a pillow for his knees. It can be visually stimulating to watch as he pleasures you.

Kneeling on your hands and knees while he pleasures you from the rear allows easy access to your vagina and anus. It is more difficult to access your clitoris, and you lose the visual stimulation. And it may be difficult to maintain this position as your arousal increases.

Pay attention to his comfort. Be sure to have plenty of pillows available to support his joints and other body parts. Make sure that you move far up enough on the bed or table so that he has enough room to get into a comfortable position. Place fresh water at the bedside in case he needs to replenish his saliva. Flavored lubricants, gels, and sauces may add spice and interest to his experience. Most women will find that they require twelve to thirty minutes or more of continuous oral stimulation to achieve the pinnacle of pleasure. You want him to stay for a while, so make him comfortable.

Communicate your needs. As with any sexual activity, communication is key. Don't expect him to intuitively know what you need. Men sometimes assume that what works for the penis will work for the clitoris. When it comes to oral pleasure, nothing could be further from the truth. The average penis likes to be sucked. Sucking the average clitoris for 5 minutes is more likely to lead to swelling and discomfort. While licking alone is unlikely to send the average penis over the top, it is exactly what the average clitoris needs. Describe for your partner exactly what you desire. It is perfectly fine to say "More to the left. Faster. Slower. Harder. More tongue." He'll be glad to know what you want him to do.

Use body language to give him feedback and direction. Move and rock your pelvis to direct his tongue to your most sensitive spots. Move side to side, thrust your pelvis closer to get more attention and farther away if the stimulation is too intense. If you want additional stimulation of your G-spot, perineum, or anus, gently guide his hands to the spot. He will soon learn exactly what you need for ultimate pleasure. *Tip:* The largest concentration of nerve endings are at the eleven and one o'clock positions along the body of the clitoris and the frenulum, the strip of tissue at the bottom of the clitoris where the labia minora meet. Ask your partner to slide his tongue from side to side over the body of your clitoris and along the frenulum to give you intense pleasure. Circular tongue motions work well here too. Strokes should be gentle in the beginning, and intensify as your arousal increases.

Vocalize your pleasure. If you are silent, he may think that you are bored, he's not doing a good job, or you have fallen asleep. Either way, he will soon lose interest in continuing cunnilingus. Moan, groan, tell him how much he is pleasing you, and let him know how it feels. He will appreciate the applause.

Give him a hand. Be an active participant. Use your fingers to pull back the hood of your clitoris, exposing the sensitive head. Stimulate your breasts, nipples, or other erogenous zones to increase your arousal. Stroke the back of his head to let him know that you are enjoying being pleasured. (But don't hold his head down, or he may have difficulty breathing.)

Kiss him immediately after cunnilingus. Taste your love juices. Kissing him lets him know that you are comfortable with your body and all of its juices.

Show appreciation. Let him know how much you enjoyed cunnilingus. Most men love to pleasure women. Knowing that he

Dr. Hil says:

So you want to try cunnilingus but are not quite sure how to broach the topic with your partner. Here are a few suggestions to get the dialogue started:

- Gently nudge his head down toward your vulva, and hope he figures it out.
- Place a trail of M&M's from your neck down to your clitoris, and offer him dessert.
- Read him a bedtime story that describes the pleasures of cunnilingus.
- Watch an educational erotic video together that illustrates the technique. My favorite is *The Complete Guide to Oral Lovemaking*. You can purchase it at www.goodvibes.com.
- Simply ask him to consider adding this technique to his sexual repertoire, and provide him with a cunnilingus handbook.

pleased you will make it more likely that he will be eager to do it again.

Remember, the pursuit of pleasure requires you to relax and see what feels good. So don't cheat yourself and your partner out of exploring cunnilingus, not just the basics, but the finer points, the subtle moves that feel *really* good. You won't be sorry.

9
. . . . .

Give the Man a Hand: Manual Pleasures

We've started to explore the paths to a woman's pleasure, but let's not forget that great, deep, satisfying sex with your partner is a two-way street. Making him feel good will make you feel good, too, especially when you're committed to having both your needs met. One fail-safe way to bring pleasure to your partner is to perform a good hand job, so let's get started on this path to *his* satisfaction.

Hand jobs. Kid stuff, you say? It is the first method most men learn to bring themselves sexual pleasure—and perhaps the first sexual move you learned as you moved to "third base" with your boyfriend in the back of the car or a dark movie theater—but it's no juvenile move. A hand job can be an important part of foreplay—a sensual warm-up to intercourse or other sexual activity—or it may be the main event. There will be times when you'll find it's the perfect way to share sexual pleasure without actually having intercourse. This familiar, comfortable technique can bring a man incredibly intense enjoyment, especially if you take the time to learn some variations on the technique. So don't underestimate the hand job. It could become your favorite sex act—and his.

Give Him a Hand

Don't just grab his crotch and start going at it. Like most women, men tend to prefer a gentle approach, at least in the beginning. Before you reach for his penis, spend some time warming him up with a sensual massage. You can invest in special massage oil (try a scented or warming oil) or use a thin, odorless cooking oil, like almond oil. Warm it slightly and place it in a dish that makes it easier to reach during the massage. (You don't want to fumble with an oily bottle while you're massaging him.)

The idea is to relax him before you excite him, so start your massage far away from his genitals. A good place to begin is his back. Place a generous amount of warm oil in the palm of your hands and begin rubbing the muscles along his spine with long, slow strokes. Start at the base of his spine, just above his buttocks and slide your hands up to his neck, out along his shoulders and back down again. With each stroke, widen the area you cover so that every inch of his back receives the warm attention of your hands. The pressure should be light; the movements slow, smooth, and continuous. Vary the type of strokes—rub upward with one hand while the other travels down; make small and large circles with both hands; or stroke outward from his spine to his sides with the palm of your hands. You don't have to knead too hard; he shouldn't feel like he's in the training room. Your focus, and his, should be on the sensuality of your touch. To make sure he knows your intentions, oil your breasts and brush them along his back, following the same path as your hands.

Continue your massage to include his arms and the backs of his legs. And don't forget his buttocks, an often neglected pleasure zone. These large muscles can carry a great deal of tension; massaging that tightness away can give him a lot of pleasure. Begin with long, firm strokes down the middle of each buttock and up the sides. Change the speed and direction of your strokes. Occasionally, let your fingers dip ever so slightly between his cheeks and brush his scrotum and anus.

Next, ask him to turn over and lie on his back so you can massage his chest. Strokes should be similar to those used on his back—long and sweeping. If he seems receptive, give a little attention to his breasts. (Some men love having their breasts massaged; others hate it. Observe his reactions for clues or ask him what he prefers.) Initial contact with his breasts should be very light. Using the tips of your fingers only, make small, delicate circles around his nipples. When they become erect, gently pinch or twiddle the nipples between your fingers. Then, using the palms of your hands, make increasingly larger circles around his breasts. Continue your massage along his shoulders and the front of his arms.

Move on to his legs, stroking his thighs, calves, and feet. When you reach his inner thighs, linger for a while. Slide your oiled fingers along this sensitive area, stopping just before you reach his genitals and moving back down his leg. With each stroke, you should get closer and closer to his scrotum until you are just brushing it. With this kind of teasing, he'll soon shudder with anticipation.

Positioning for a Hand Job

The key to making sure he gets a satisfying hand job is to make sure you *both* are comfortable. He should be in a position where he can relax; you should be able to switch hand positions or move around

Is He in Good Hands?

Before you go for his groin, take a minute and look at your hands. They should be free of any areas that might cause pain or injury to your partner's sensitive genitals. Though the penis can appear to be tough and hard, the skin down there is actually thin and sensitive. With that in mind, be sure that your nails are well trimmed, without sharp or jagged edges. Check your hands for dry, scratchy areas or calluses. Hands that are soft and smooth provide the best sensual pleasure. Remove all rings that might injure him. Also make sure your hands are warm. Few things kill an erection like icy fingers, so warm them up by rubbing them together or holding them under warm running water.

You can give a hand job with unlubricated hands—some men like the extra friction created as two dry surfaces rub against each other—but most guys prefer the warm, wet sensation of a lubricant. By lubricant, I mean almost anything wet or oily; you can experiment to see what he likes best and what lasts longest. Petroleum jelly is what many men use when they masturbate, so it's an obvious choice if you want to re-create the sensations that he is most familiar with. But don't use it if you're going to use a condom afterward; it can weaken the structure of the latex and cause it to break. You can use simple household cooking oil or baby oil; these are thin and smooth and convenient. (Again, skip these if you'll be using a condom later.) Regular moisturizing lotions can be used in a pinch, but they don't last very long. And you'll want to make sure they're not laced with fragrances or chemicals that will irritate his skin down there. Likewise, saliva is a great lubricant but does not last more than a few minutes. It may be in your best interest to invest in a

❧ *continued*

water-based lubricant. You can find a basic formula at any drugstore; hit your local sex shop or condom boutique for fancy flavored ones. The very best lubes for a hand job are those that contain silicone: Eros Bodyglide and Wet Platinum are two brands you might look for. They last a very long time and create sensations similar to those created during intercourse.

as needed to get the job done with ease. The latter is important. It usually takes longer for a man to come with a hand job than the few minutes it takes for him to orgasm during intercourse, so you don't want your arm to get tired or your hand to cramp at an inopportune time.

Some positions that work include:

- He lies on his back, legs spread apart. You kneel between his legs, facing him. This places your thumbs in position for you to stroke his frenulum easily.
- He lies on his back. You straddle his torso with your back to him, facing his penis. If you don't weigh much and he has strong abs, you can sit, at least for a while. But if you're heavy, you'll need to support your weight on your knees.
- He lies on his back. You kneel on either side of his torso or hips. Just don't rest your elbow on his body.
- He stands. You sit on the bed or a chair.
- He stands. You stand behind him and reach around his body to his penis.
- He stands or sits. You kneel in front of him. Put a pillow under your knees for comfort.

ॐ You lie on your back with your head on pillows. He straddles your chest, supporting his weight on his knees.

ॐ You both lie on your sides facing each other. You reach down between his legs. This is an intimate position that allows you to kiss and look into each other's eyes. He can also reach over and stimulate your clitoris at the same time (mutual masturbation).

ॐ He lies on his side. You lie behind him in the spooning position so that your dominant hand can reach over his body to grasp his penis.

Hand Job 101: The Basic Stroke

Begin by getting into position. A good beginner position is the one in which you kneel between his legs. Make sure your hands are warm and well lubricated, then cup them just over his genitals, close but not quite touching. Give him time to feel the warmth and flow of energy from your hands. Now slowly lower your hands until you are lightly touching him, covering his penis and scrotum. Let your hands rest here for a few seconds before moving on.

Wrap the slightly opened fist of your dominant hand around the shaft of his penis, with your thumb on the underside (along the ridge in the back). Place the thumb and index finger of your other hand at the base of his penis to stabilize it. Begin to gently but firmly slide your fist up and down the shaft. When you slide up, tighten your grip slightly as your hand comes up over the head. Then slide all the way down to the base of his penis. Continue with a smooth, steady rhythm: up, down, up, down. Begin slowly and increase speed gradually as you notice him getting harder or reacting with more excitement. He'll give you signs that he wants more intensity.

Variations for More Pleasure

That simple movement may be all he needs to experience a wonderfully powerful orgasm. But as you both get more comfortable with the basic stroke, you might explore the following moves.

- Begin with the basic stroke. As you slowly slide your hand up and down his penis, move your thumb rapidly, up and down or in circles, against the underside and frenulum (the sensitive web of tissue on the back of the penis where the shaft meets the head) of his penis. Make sure your thumb is well lubricated to make rapid movement easier.
- Begin with the basic stroke. When your hand reaches the head of the penis, twist your hand in one direction and then continue down to the base of his penis.
- Begin with the basic stroke. When your hand reaches the head, twist the palm of your hand completely over the head of his penis as if you are rubbing it and then continue with the downstroke.
- With your thumb and index finger, make an "okay" sign. Slide the "O" over the head of his penis and move it up and down the shaft. After a while, lengthen your stroke. Tighten your grip as you near the corona of the head. Then slide your fingers up and over the head, then back down again.
- Start with the same "okay" movement as above, but when you slide your index finger and thumb up to the head, twist your fingers in each direction a few times along the corona (the rim of the head), before sliding down to the base again.
- While his penis is lying against his abdomen, place your thumb and index finger at the base of his penis to stabilize it. Lubricate the palm of your dominant hand and slide it up and down the back of his penis. To add interest, you can slide one hand down

his scrotum to his perineum while the other hand slides up along his penis. (Your hands will be moving in opposite directions.)

ဆ Wrap your hand around his penis, with your thumb at the base of his penis and your pinkie resting near the head. (Your hand is essentially "upside down.") Now slide your hand up and down. This technique works best if you are kneeling at his side.

ဆ Cup the head of his penis in the palm of your hand, with your fingers pointing down toward his scrotum. Grip the sides of his penis and rotate the palm of your hand in one direction and then the other.

ဆ Circle the base of his penis with the thumb and index finger of your nondominant hand. Pull downward, pulling the skin of his penis taut. Now wrap your well-lubricated dominant hand around the shaft and head, and slowly stroke up and down. Holding the skin taut will increase his sensations.

Dr. Hil says:

If there's one technique that every woman needs to master, it's the hand job. With this method, you can bring intense pleasure to your partner anytime and almost anywhere. You can make it part of your sexual foreplay to add variety to your sex life. It's also a great technique to use when he wants sex and you don't or can't. And why not? It's so easy to learn. With a little practice (try it on a dildo until your movements are continuous and smooth) and mastery of a variety of moves, you'll soon be curling his toes with pleasure.

Hand Job 201: Using Both Hands

- Place both well-lubricated fists around his penis, one on top of the other. Move your hands in unison up and down the entire length of his penis. He'll get a sensation similar to thrusting into a long, tight vagina.

- Place both hands as above, but as you move them up and down, twist both hands together in one direction and then in the other. Add more interest by twisting one hand in one direction and the other in the opposite direction.

- Lace the fingers of both hands together and encircle his penis. Your thumbs should be free, positioned at the level of the frenulum. Now, keeping your hands still, move just your thumbs up and down in opposite directions along the frenulum, varying the speed and pressure.

- Interlock your hands as above, but lace your thumbs together as well. Slide your interlocked hands up and down his penis.

- Grasp the head of his penis with your right hand and slide it down to the base. When you reach the base, place your left hand on the head and slide it down. Release your right hand and return to the head. Repeat with alternating hands.

- Grasp the head of his penis with your right hand and use the same alternating technique as above, except slide only your right hand down to just below the head before you start with the left. Alternate hands for several rapid strokes. This technique works best with an erect penis.

- This technique is the opposite of the one above. Place your right hand around the base of his penis and slide it up and over the head. As you reach the head, begin the same upward movement with your left hand. Repeat with alternating hands.

❧ Same as above, except each hand begins just below the head and slides up over the head and back down to an inch or two below it. Repeat for several rapid strokes before returning to the longer strokes described above. This technique may be used on a flaccid penis, but don't expect it to remain flaccid for long!

❧ Form an "okay" sign with the thumb and index finger of each hand. Place both "O's" around his penis. Now slide one hand up and just over the corona, while moving the other down to the base of the penis. Move both O's back and forth. Add interest by twisting your hands as they move up and down.

❧ Kneel between his legs. Hold his penis between the palms of your hands, with fingers straight along both sides of his penis. Now slowly and gently slap his penis from side to side between your hands. Watch for his reaction; some men love this, but others hate it. If he's into it, gradually increase the speed and intensity of the movement. This works best for the man whose penis points straight out or slightly down when erect.

❧ Place the palms of your hands on both sides of his penis. Gently rub your hands back and forth, in opposite directions, along the side of his penis as if starting a fire like a Girl Scout.

❧ Place the palms of your hands on both sides of his penis. Rub your hands in opposite directions up and down the full length of his penis: as one goes up, the other goes down.

Advanced Hand Techniques

Once you get comfortable with giving a hand job and you've explored the variations described earlier in this chapter, you may want to move on to more complicated positions. Try anything that suits your interest, agility, and comfort level. And if any of these moves seem too complex or strenuous, just try something else. After all, this is supposed to be fun for both of you.

Ten Keys to a Great Hand Job

1. The very best way to learn how to give your man pleasure is to learn how he pleasures himself. Ask him to show you his own moves. If he's too shy for show-and-tell, ask him to place your hand the way he likes it on his penis. Then have him put his hand over yours and show you which movements and how much pressure and speed give him the most pleasure. Of course, once you learn some of the techniques in this chapter you'll be doing things he might never have imagined for himself, but it helps to start with what he knows to be pleasurable.

2. Show some enthusiasm. Let him know that you're excited about giving him pleasure.

3. Honor his penis. Tell him how much you like looking at it and playing with it. Let him know you love it soft, hard, or anything in between. Don't pressure him to have an erection; he will receive pleasure even if it is soft, and his pleasure is all that matters when it comes to a hand job.

4. Focus all your attention on him. This is no time for daydreaming. Manually stimulating your partner is an unselfish gesture of love. Focus on his reactions and the pleasure that you are providing. Take your time and savor every moment.

5. Communication is very important. Ask him to let you know when you are hitting the right spots and, more important, when you *aren't*.

6. Begin slowly with a gentle touch.

7. Choose a great lubricant.

continued

8. Use both hands. When stimulating his penis with one hand, the other shouldn't lie idle. Cup or stroke his scrotum, perineum, or anus. Reach up and massage his lower abdomen or nipples. Stroke his inner thighs.

9. Vary your hand motions. If you continue one stroke for too long, his penis will lose its sensitivity and become numb.

10. Continue to stimulate him as he comes, if he likes that. Some men become supersensitive after ejaculation and don't like to have their penis touched afterward. Others like to be stimulated until the very last drop of semen has been released. Watch his reaction for cues, or simply ask what he prefers.

❧ He gets in the doggy position on hands and knees. You kneel behind him and reach between his legs. Stroke his scrotum, then wrap your dominant hand around his penis. Begin the basic up-and-down stroke. As he becomes aroused, plant kisses all over his buttocks and, if you are flexible, his anus and scrotum. This technique is guaranteed to be memorable.

❧ From a position that allows you to face him, begin with the basic stroke. As he becomes aroused, place your mouth over just the head of his penis with your lips fitting snuggly in the groove beneath the corona. Continue to stroke with your hand, while flicking the tip of the head with your tongue.

❧ He lies on his back as you begin the basic stroke or one of its variations. While stroking with one hand, reach for a well-lubricated penis sleeve with the other. (See "Boy Toys" in chapter 15.) Slide the sleeve over his erect penis and move it up and down, using the basic stroke. The sleeve creates a sensation much like a vagina; he'll love it.

- Place several small marbles in a glass of warm water. Have him lie on his back as you begin the basic stroke. As he becomes aroused, slip a small marble into your palm and continue stroking his penis. The marble will move smoothly along his penis adding another layer of sensation. As you become more comfortable manipulating one marble, you can add one or two more. Keep your grip light to allow the marbles to move. Grip too hard, and you may hurt him.

- Place a large latex or plastic glove on your dominant hand. Lubricate it well, then hold his penis in your hand and begin the basic up-and-down or any of the variations. The excess material of the glove will stimulate every inch of his penis as you stroke.

- Prepare a warm bath for him, adding a moisturizing bath oil or baby oil to the water. As he soaks, kneel at the side of the tub, reach into the water, and begin to massage and stroke his penis. The warmth of the water increases blood flow to his penis, and the water itself acts as a good lubricant, making your hand movements easier. If you like, you can change the sensation a bit by lubricating your hand with a long-lasting lubricant that is stable underwater, like Eros Bodyglide. Or add more excitement by slipping in the tub behind him and reaching around his body to stroke his penis. The feel of your naked breasts and pelvis against his skin will drive him nuts.

- Slip a finger vibrator on the middle finger of your nondominant hand. While stroking his penis with your dominant hand, cup your other hand gently over his scrotum and press the vibrating finger against his perineum. The vibrations will spread to his G-spot and drive him wild.

- Place a hand vibrator on the back of your dominant hand. Lubricate your palm and slide your hand up and down the shaft of his penis. With every two or three up strokes, slide your hand over the head of his penis and then back down the shaft.

∽ Stroke his penis up and down with your nondominant hand. Meanwhile, place a hand warmer (the kind you use to warm your hands while skiing) in your dominant hand until it's quite warm. Now thoroughly moisten your warm hand with warm oil and wrap it around his penis. The extra heat will surprise him and add another dimension to his pleasure.

∽ Place a cock ring at the base of his erect penis. Begin with the basic one-hand technique and advance to any of the single-hand variations. As he nears ejaculation, remove your hand and wait for his arousal to subside just a bit. Now place both hands around his penis and use any of the two-hand techniques. As he nears orgasm again, remove your hands for few seconds. Now use his favorite hand technique to once again bring him to the brink. This time, just as he is about to ejaculate, remove the cock ring and let it spurt.

∽ Kneel between his legs, as he lies on his back with his knees bent. Prop his buttocks on a pillow or two so that his pelvis is slightly elevated. Stroke his penis with your nondominant hand. Use the well-lubricated middle finger of your dominant hand to begin to massage his anus. Slowly, gently apply more pressure to his anus until it becomes more relaxed, then push your finger deeper. Don't rush; take the time to check his reaction. If he seems to be resisting, back off. But if he's enjoying it, push farther into his anus and, curving your finger in a "come here" motion, begin to stroke the front wall just below his prostate gland. The gland will feel like a firm bulge about the size of a walnut. Your movements should be gentle, yet firm, and slow. All the while, you continue to stroke his penis.*

*NOTE: If you are planning to enter his anus, trim your nails and file any jagged edges until smooth. Long nails and tips may injure his delicate tissues and require medical attention.

❧ He stands while you sit on the bed or a chair. Lubricate both of your hands well with warm oil or silicone-based lubricant. Form a barrel by making two open fists and placing one hand on top of the other. Slide the barrel over his penis and remain still. Let him thrust his penis in and out of the barrel. To add variety, squeeze his penis tight as he pulls back and loosen your hands as he thrusts forward. You can also squeeze and release your fingers rhythmically to create sensations similar to those you create when you squeeze your PC muscle (practice Kegel exercises) during intercourse.

Exploring and practicing the art of the hand job will make you *both* feel good. It's an essential skill every woman needs to master.

10

. . . . .

The Pleasures of Fellatio

Ask a group of men to name the one sexual pleasure that they don't get enough of, and chances are very good that most will say "fellatio." (Well, they'll say "blow job" or use another less clinical term.) The fact is, men absolutely love receiving oral sex. It's easy to imagine why. While being inside your soft, warm, wet vagina is pleasurable, your soft, warm, wet mouth is much more versatile. Using your lips, mouth, and tongue, you can create a multitude of pleasurable sensations for him that can't be duplicated any other way. You can dance around his most sensitive parts with your tongue. By guiding his penis with your hands and applying a certain amount of pressure with your mouth, you can control the depth of penetration. You can apply varying degrees of suction and even create vibrations by humming or making sounds in your throat. All that, plus your hands are free to stimulate his penis, scrotum, and the rest of his body as far as you can reach.

Unlike intercourse, fellatio gives him no need to worry about his performance. (In fact, he doesn't even have to have an erection to receive oral pleasure.) When you perform oral sex on your man, he can just lie back and enjoy himself. And since he doesn't have to work, he can surrender to the feeling and focus more intently on the pleasurable sensations you're giving him. Because he can be so totally into it, his orgasm may be more intense than one he'd achieve through intercourse.

Then there are the psychological reasons men like having oral sex performed on them. For some men, the penis is a symbol of manhood; a woman who goes down on him "bestows honor" on his penis and acknowledges his masculinity. Many men say that fellatio makes them feel loved and special, and some even consider it to be more intimate than intercourse. After all, he is trusting you with his most prized possession between your teeth!

If you learn how to provide your man with oral pleasure, it not only makes him happy but can relieve you of some performance pressure as well. When you prefer not to have intercourse—you're tired, you're having your period, you've got a yeast infection, or you're just not in the mood—you can still have a wonderfully sexy and satisfying time with him. And, while oral sex without a condom isn't safe sex, you can't get pregnant going down on a man, so it's a good option when you don't have adequate birth control.

But it's not just a when-all-else-fails technique, and it's not just for his pleasure. Some women get a lot of pleasure of their own through performing fellatio. The sight of your partner's genitals in a state of sexual arousal—the fact that he's turned on by you—can be very sexy. It can make *you* feel powerful and in control. Some women are even able to climax from the intense emotional and physical aspects of fellatio and the fantasies they associate with it. So don't shy away from it; instead, I encourage you to master the art of fellatio and reap the pleasures it will reward you both.

Oral Objections (His and Yours)

While most men relish the thought of oral sex, some do shy away from it. And even if your man doesn't, it may bring up a few feelings of insecurity for him. Like women, men don't always find it easy to relax when you are up so close and personal with his genitals. It may sound silly, but he may worry about whether you approve of his penis or not. Do you find it attractive? Is it large enough to meet your standards? Did you notice that it curves to one side? Does he smell down there? Are you turned off by his scent or his taste? Are you freaked out by his uncircumcised penis? Is it hard enough? Will it stay hard enough? These are some of the thoughts that may be flashing through his mind, even as he's enjoying the best blow job of his life.

But you understand sexual insecurity. It's very easy to feel inadequate when you're naked and vulnerable and can't hide any self-perceived flaws in your anatomy. Be sensitive to any insecurities he may have. While you're down there, make sure you let him know that you like what you see, hear, touch, smell, and taste. And let him know that the only thing you're thinking about is giving him pleasure.

Know, too, that his reluctance may be less physical than psychological. If your man has gotten negative messages about sex and sexuality, accepting pleasure can sometimes be difficult, blocked by feelings of guilt and shame. A sexual technique like fellatio, perhaps more than "regular" sex, may bring some of these feelings to the surface. Communication is key here. Make a point of talking about any negative feelings he might have, but don't start grilling him while you're about to go down on him. Pick a relaxed time when you're not in the throes of passion and see if you can get him to open up.

While you're talking, tell him about any misgivings *you* may have about oral sex. Many women have them. For some of us it's the guilt factor. We think giving head is degrading and only bad girls and prostitutes engage in such activities. But fellatio is simply another way to bring your man pleasure, no better and no worse than intercourse. Think about it: What would make it okay for a man to enter your vagina—your most private area—but not okay for him to enter your mouth? And remember: He's sensitive about this stuff. He may assume that you find his genitals—an important part of him— disgusting or unacceptable. He may interpret your refusal to give him oral pleasure as a rejection of his penis and, by extension, him and his manhood.

For some of us, it's not that we don't want to do it; it's that we're afraid we don't know how to do it right and won't risk the embarrassment. That's what this chapter is for. Like any other sexual technique, good fellatio can, and must, be learned. Once you read this chapter, you can become an oral expert. If you want to make his toes curl and increase the chance that he will work hard to do the same for you, it's worth learning how to perform fellatio and to do it well.

Dr. Hil says:

If you care about your man, the question should not be *whether* you give him oral pleasure but *how often*. He should not have to beg for it or expect it only on special occasions. And you shouldn't do it out of obligation or to stop his whining about it. If you are really into *him,* you should really get into *it.* Take the time to learn the steps, practice to perfect your signature technique, and approach it with enthusiasm and care. But if you just can't stomach it for whatever reason, let it go and find another sexual technique that you can really enjoy.

And Why Not?

Part of our problem with oral sex is that some of us can't seem to get past the "ick" factor. Fellatio puts you face-to-face with a man's nether region, and some women are, frankly, nervous about the encounter. Let's eliminate some of the myths that might be holding you back.

He might smell. Unless he has poor hygiene habits, the scent of his genitals shouldn't be unpleasant. In fact, the slight musky scent of a man's crotch can be an arousing olfactory aphrodisiac. If you are concerned about his odor, you can suggest that the two of you begin sex play with a shower. Soap him up with your hands, feeling and fondling his genitals. With the combination of warm water and your soft hands, he'll be hard before you know it; you two may not make it out of the shower.

I might not like the taste. What taste? There shouldn't really be much of one, since the penis is covered with the same skin that covers the rest of his body. If he has perspired down there, it might taste a little salty, but no more so than, say, his neck. Once he's fully aroused, he may release small amounts of clear fluid, the so-called pre-cum, but that too has very little taste. It may be slightly salty or a little sweet, but rarely is it unpleasant. If you allow him to ejaculate in your mouth, you may encounter more of a taste from his semen, again ranging from salty to sweet to neutral. But this will vary from one man to another and in the same man at different times.

He might pee. While it's true that urine and semen travel down the same tube, the urethra, and exit from the same hole in the penis, they don't—and can't—travel at the same time. And it is impossible for a man to urinate when he has his hard penis in your mouth.

I might gag. You won't if you learn proper oral sex techniques. Four tips: Use your hands to control the depth of penetration of his penis. Exhale as you insert his penis into your mouth. Keep his penis in the center of your mouth as it nears the back of your throat. Don't *anticipate* gagging. Instead, concentrate on the pleasure you are giving and receiving.

I might hurt him or damage his penis. Again, proper technique is key. Wrap your lips around your teeth to avoid damage to his skin. Believe me, if it hurts he will not be a silent martyr!

Start with Good Positioning

Before you get into the groove, you've got to get into position. That's one of the most important aspects of performing oral sex. To make sure you're able to go the distance, you need to consider your comfort and his as well as his anatomy.

First, you need to be as comfortable as possible. When he's writhing and moaning, just about to explode with pleasure, you certainly don't want to have to stop what you're doing because you have a cramp in your neck. Make sure you're in a position that you can stay in for a while or that you can move around in without losing either your rhythm or good contact with his penis. If you're constantly shifting, it'll be a distraction to him and to you, and you'll never reach your goal. Also, choose a position that allows you to continue to have complete control of the depth of penetration of his penis. You'll be much more comfortable if you can decide where, when, and how far he enters.

You also want him to be comfortable. (This is his treat, after all.) He should be able to relax and enjoy himself without any discomfort or distraction. In most cases he'll probably be lying or sitting down, so fellatio shouldn't be a strain on his stamina. But you want to choose your own positions such that you can support yourself without putting too much weight on him. Avoid positions that require you to rest your arm and elbow on his hips or legs.

Also consider his particular anatomy when you decide to go down on him. If his penis points up and lies against his abdomen when he is erect, choose a position that doesn't require you to pull his penis down to get it into your mouth. Likewise, if he points to the left or right when he's erect, approach him from the side that places less stress on his penis.

Another trick of the trade: Men are visual; they get turned on by what they see as well as by what they feel. For maximum impact, get into a position that allows him a clear view of the action. If you have long hair, you might want to pin it up or tie it back so that he can watch you put his penis into your mouth, see you fondle and stroke him, and observe your expressions of pleasure. Fellatio is not an activity to be done in the dark or under the covers. To enhance the mood and make for a more arousing, erotic experience, use dim lighting or place candles strategically around the room. He'll be able to watch you worship his penis, which may be his biggest turn-on.

Fellatio 101

Great oral sex begins behind his ear. Yes, you heard me correctly. You should begin kissing, sucking, licking, and nuzzling as far away from his penis as is possible and slowly, carefully, skillfully work your way south. Though he may get an erection within seconds of realizing what you have in mind, you need to take your time and bring him to a complete state of arousal before you even put your mouth to his member. This teasing will increase his pleasure and make his orgasm much more intense. (And what's good for the goose. . . . This will go a long way toward showing your man how he should pleasure you.)

So, where were we? You are slowly working your way from his ear down his neck, shoulders, and back, undressing him piece by piece as you move down his body. Moisten your lips and plant kisses along his spine from his neck to his coccyx, the sexy triangle right where his butt cheeks meet. Linger there for a while before moving back up his spine slowly, tracing it with your tongue. Kiss along his neck, his shoulder blades, his pecs (chest muscles), and make whatever adjustment you need to to be able to fondle his breasts. Take his nipples into your mouth and swirl your tongue around them one at a time.

Move down his chest to his abdomen, kissing and nuzzling. Stick your tongue in his navel and lick it. Lick your way down his lower abdomen to his pubic hair line. Linger here for a minute, then nibble and suck your way down his inner thighs, skipping his genitals entirely. Use your tongue to lick a path back up to where his thighs meet his genital area. Spend a while here to increase his anticipation, letting your cheek or your hair brush his penis a little.

At this point, he may be starting to beg and moving his pelvis toward your mouth. Resist the urge to take him into your mouth a little longer. Instead, move your mouth to the spot right over but not touching his penis. With your mouth open, your lips forming an "O," blow warm air over his penis and scrotum. Extend your very wet tongue and slowly lick him from his perineum (the strip between the base of the penis and the anus) to the tip of his penis in one continuous movement. When you reach the top, blow air through pursed lips from the tip back down to the perineum. Your breath will feel cool on his skin.

Spend a couple of minutes applying long, slow, wet licks from his perineum or anus, over his scrotum, along the scrotal raphe (the seam down the middle of the scrotum), and the entire length of his penis to the head, then back down again. Swirl your outstretched tongue around the head of the penis and corona (the rim around the head).

Finally, slowly slide his penis into your mouth. Make sure that you cover your teeth with your lips to avoid scraping his penis. Take as much as you can into your mouth and then . . . don't move. Relax.

Use your tongue to press his penis into the roof of your mouth. Now slowly slide your mouth up and down his penis. Your lips should form a nice, comfortable, gentle seal around the penis. This is a good time to make eye contact with him to let him know that you are enjoying this as much as he is.

To increase his stimulation and control the depth of penetration, hold him at the base of his penis by making a ring with your thumb and one or more fingers of one hand. As your mouth moves up and down, let your hand follow, as an extension of your mouth. Working in harmony, your mouth and hand will make it feel almost as if he is very deep inside your vagina.

Lubrication is very important at this point. If you can produce enough saliva to keep your hands and your mouth moist, you're golden. Otherwise, have a good water-based lubricant on hand, a flavored one or a plain formula with a tolerable taste. Apply it to his penis and to your hand to make sure your hand slides as effortlessly as your mouth.

Begin the blow job with movements as slow and careful as your earlier kissing, then gradually increase the pace. You might also vary your tempo by moving rapidly in and out for a few strokes, then slowly for an equal number. Vary the depth of penetration: Sometimes just take in the head; other times, the entire penis or some point in between. Be creative and mix it up. If you keep him guessing, you'll also keep him interested. The simple up-and-down movement is enough to bring some men to climax. When that happens, you'll know you've passed Fellatio 101.

But do you want him to just experience an orgasm? Or do you want him to have a memorable experience? If it's the latter, you should read on. Fellatio 201 will give you more tips and techniques that will help you create your own signature fellatio style, one that will make him think of you whenever he hears the term *blow job*. With that in mind, try all of the different techniques that follow. Mix and match. Be creative. Discover what works best for both of you.

Other Positions to Explore

He lies flat; you kneel. This is perhaps the easiest position and the most comfortable for both of you. From his reclined position, he can totally relax and be in a better state to receive pleasure; and he can elevate his head on a pillow or two, to have a better view of the action. You're kneeling between his knees, facing him, which allows your mouth and tongue the best access to the most sensitive underside of his penis. Your hands are free to roam his scrotum, buttocks, the inside of his thighs, and his nipples.

If his penis points up and against his abdomen, lean forward to get the right angle and prevent bending his penis back too far. Use your arms and hands to support your body weight; don't lean your elbow on his abdomen or pelvis.

He lies; you lie. You're on your stomach, down between his legs, facing him. This position works well for the man that points down when he's erect, but it limits your hand movements, so you can't easily explore his other erogenous zones. It can also put stress on your neck. Put pillows under your upper body for support.

He lies flat; you straddle his chest. You're facing his penis with your back to him. It's a different angle and, therefore, provides different sensations for him. He's also got a good view of your back side, a real turn-on for some men. You have good access to his corona (rim of the penis) but not to his frenulum (the sensitive web in the back). With good lip action, you can compensate, though.

He lies propped up; you straddle his chest. This is a version of the 69 position. It's the same as above, except that you slide your pelvis back to give his mouth access to your vulva and clitoris. While the concept of mutual pleasuring sounds great, it may be quite difficult to focus on pleasuring him when your own pleasure begins to peak.

He lies; you kneel beside him. This is good for the man whose penis points more to one side or the other when erect. So if he points to the right, you'll want to kneel on his right side and vice versa. But this is also a good choice for any guy just for a change of pace. The sensations he feels when his penis is inserted at an angle are different and interesting. Again use your arms and hands to support your body weight.

He stands; you sit. Perch yourself on the bed or a chair facing him. This position allows you free access to let your hands roam, and, unless he gets tired of standing or you make him too weak in the knees, it's a comfortable position for both of you.

He sits; you kneel. Rest your knees on a pillow in front of him. It's physically comfortable for both of you, but some women don't like this position because it is one often assumed in porn films. Some guys like it for the very same reason. Think of it as just another option for lovemaking and pleasuring your partner.

You lie on your back; he straddles your chest. Prop your head on a pillow or two, and let him put his penis into your mouth. This position doesn't give you as much control of the action. He may insert his penis too deeply or thrust too fast and make you gag. It may be okay for a quickie if you communicate with him before you get started.

You both lie on your sides. You're facing each other, with his genitals at the level of your mouth. At least one hand is free to caress him. Prop your head on pillows to decrease the strain on your neck.

You lie down on the bed with your head hanging over the side. He stands at the bedside. From this position, he inserts his penis. This is the position made popular by Linda Lovelace in the movie *Deep Throat*. Few women would find this one comfortable or be able to sustain a prolonged fellatio session this way. This is more of a novelty position, something to try before you move on to another position.

Fellatio 201: Advanced Techniques

Now that you know how to approach your man, how to position yourself, and how to give him oral pleasure of the basic kind, it's time to move on to the next level. There's so much more you can do to bring him pleasure. If you learn these techniques, you'll be able to offer him hours and hours of satisfaction. He'll never be bored. In fact, he'll be so enthralled with you, he'll keep coming back for more.

Heading in the Right Direction

- Wrap your lips around the head of his penis, so that your lips fit snugly around the base of his head, enveloping the corona, or rim. Lay your flat tongue against the penis, pressing it against the roof of your mouth. The pressure of your lips should be moderately snug. Now move your head slowly from side to side, as if saying "no." Your lips will massage his corona. Vary the speed. As he shows signs of pleasure, plunge your mouth down rapidly, taking in as much of the penis as you can without gagging. (Watch your teeth; don't scratch him.) This surprise is sure to get a moan out of him. Then return to the head and the side-to-side massages.
- As you slide your mouth up and down his penis, twist your head in corkscrew fashion.

Give Him a Hand

- Take his penis in your hands. Playfully slap or rub it along the side of your face, your lips, and nose while he watches.
- Place both hands around the shaft of the penis, one on top of the other. Place your mouth on the head. Move the hands up and down in sync with your mouth.
- Put both hands on the shaft and twist them in opposite directions as you move them up or down the shaft in sync with your mouth. Be gentle and make sure your hands are well lubricated.
- As you slide your mouth up the shaft, twist your mouth and hands to one side or the other. Twist in the opposite direction as you move down the shaft. Alternatively, you can twist your head in one direction and your hand in the other.
- While sliding his penis in and out of your mouth, pull down on the skin of his penis with one hand and hold it taut. Stretching the skin will increase the sensations he feels while you lick, suck, and swallow his penis.
- Place one hand at the base of his penis and your mouth above your hand. Let your hand and mouth work in concert: as your mouth moves up, your hand follows. When you reach the head, your mouth slides off, while your hand goes up and over the top of the head and back down. Your mouth follows. Repeat.

Tongue in Groove

The tongue is the key to ultimate oral sex. In fact, nothing enlivens fellatio like an active tongue. Your tongue should be in constant motion, up and down, side to side, diagonally, figure eights, and circles.

- Flick the entire penis lightly with the tip of your tongue, slowly, then rapidly.

- Rim the *sulcus* (the groove between the shaft and the rim) of the penis with the tip of your tongue, then with your flat, relaxed tongue.

- Use the tip of your tongue to flick the opening of the *urethra,* the tiny opening at the top of the head.

- While moving your mouth up and down the shaft of the penis, move your tongue slowly and rapidly from side to side against the *frenulum* (the sensitive web of tissue on the back of the penis where the shaft meets the head).

- While moving your mouth up and down his shaft, circle the head with your tongue.

- Slide as much of his penis as you can comfortably into your mouth. Now curl your tongue up and toward the back of your throat repeatedly in a lapping motion.

- Extend your flat tongue and slide the head of his penis across it.

- Place your lips on either side of the *corpus spongiosum,* the spongy tube that forms a ridge on the back of the penis. Slide your lips up and down the shaft, along this ridge. Flick your tongue and kiss his penis as you move up and down.

- Using your flat, soft tongue, begin at the *scrotal raphe* (the seam down the middle of the scrotum) and lick up to the base of the penis, then across, circling around one testicle and back to the raphe. Then lick up, over, and around the other testicle and back to the raphe, creating a figure eight. Repeat. Add interest by using your pointed, firm tongue. Then repeat with a flicking tongue, up and down, then side to side.

Get the Sensation

- Studies have shown that when people are blindfolded, their sense of touch becomes stronger. With this in mind, place a loose blindfold over his eyes before giving head. This adds an element of surprise because he won't be able to predict your next move.

∞ With his penis snug in your mouth, begin to moan deeply. The vibrations you create will spread all along his penis, giving him a new sensation.

∞ Insert his penis all the way into your mouth. As you move up and down on his penis, suck air through the sides of your moist mouth to create an erotic slurping sound.

∞ Place a piece of ice in the hollow of you cheek. Now insert the penis into your otherwise warm mouth. The hot/cold sensation will be exciting.

∞ Have a bowl of frozen melon balls nearby. Place a couple in your mouth before you slide the penis in. The soft texture combined with the cold temperature of the melon may be very stimulating.

∞ Sip herbal tea—just enough to warm your mouth—before sliding his penis into your mouth. (Coffee or black tea will dehydrate you. You don't want a dry mouth during oral sex.) Alternately, hold a mouthful of the warm (not hot) drink, then slide the penis in and swish the liquid from one cheek to the other. Swallow before you continue oral pleasuring.

∞ Slip a very strong breath mint, like an Altoid, into your mouth. As it begins to melt, slide his penis into your mouth. Some men find the sensation—a combination of tingling, hot, and cold—incredible.

∞ Cover his penis and scrotum with flavored gels, creams, chocolate sauce, or whipped cream, then lick and suck it off. (Be sure that all of it is removed before putting his penis in your vagina. You may want to wash or cover it with a condom to decrease your risk of a vaginal infection.)

∞ Place a few pieces of Pop Rocks candy into the hollow of your cheek. As it starts to fizz, slide his penis in and out of your mouth. The popping candy will add a bit of excitement. Don't place the candy directly on his penis, however, as the sensation may be too intense, even painful.

℞ Fill your mouth with champagne before inserting his penis. The bubbles will provide a sizzling sensation.

℞ Place a large spoon of mashed banana or applesauce in your mouth. Slide the penis in and slowly move the head in and out of your mouth. The feel of the soft fruit will drive him mad.

Surprise, Surprise

℞ Almost every man will tell you that teeth are a no-no during fellatio. However, there are a few who admit that they enjoy very light stroking of the penis with their partner's teeth. Before trying this move, ask your partner about preference.

℞ Wake him up in the middle of the night by taking his penis completely in your mouth and sucking gently.

℞ While he is still in his boxers or briefs, drop to your knees and kiss his penis through the fabric. Then take the rising penis into your mouth and suck through the fabric. The message is "I can't wait to give you pleasure. I want you so much that I can't wait for you to fully undress."

Extracurriculars

℞ Lick and suck his perineum while your hands slide up and down his penis. It may help to prop his buttocks on pillows to make it easier to access his bottom.

℞ Sit in a chair and let him stand in front of you. Put lubricant in your cleavage and place his penis between your breasts, pressing them together to enclose his penis. As he slides in and out, extend your tongue and flick the head as it exits.

℞ Slide his penis into your mouth, angling it toward your cheek. Place a battery-powered vibrator outside your cheek and let him feel the vibrations.

- Restrain his hands with novelty handcuffs or a lightly tied silk scarf as you perform oral pleasures. It adds an aspect of fantasy to your pleasuring.

- Pretend that his perineum is your clitoris and lick it the way that you like to be licked. Believe me, he will remember this the next time that he goes down on you!

- Spend some time licking his anus, a practice called *analingus*. Make sure he's thoroughly clean, then use your pointed tongue to lick in a slow, then rapid, motion. Flick your tongue in side-to-side, up-and-down, and circular patterns. (Be aware that some men don't like anal sex play, so if he resists or stiffens, move on. You can also ask, but we don't want to turn oral sex into 20 Questions.) Note: If you are not sure of his health status, it's a good idea to use a dental dam, a condom that has been cut open, or a piece of plastic wrap over the anus during analingus to protect yourself from hepatitis, parasites, and sexually transmitted infections.

- Lie between his legs as he lies on his back. Place both hands on his thighs and push them up toward his chest or you can place his legs on your shoulders. Begin at the base of his buttocks and lick with your pointed tongue in a zigzag, all the way up to the head of his penis. Repeat with your flat tongue in a figure-eight pattern.

- While sliding his penis in and out of your mouth, place lubricant on your fingers and massage his anus. If he seems interested, you can gently slip a finger inside and massage his sacred spot.

- Open your mouth wide and gently envelop one of his testicles with your warm mouth. Don't suck; just flick or swirl it with your tongue. Give special attention to the line down the center, the scrotal raphe. (Some men hate to have their testes sucked. Ask him before you try this move.)

Getting in Deep

- Suction can create interesting sensations. Suck while sliding your mouth up and down on the penis.
- Slide the penis halfway into your mouth. Apply suction as you move up the penis, stopping when you reach just beneath the head. Then increase suction and pop the head out of your mouth. The sound alone will make him moan.
- Insert just the head of his penis into your mouth and slide it in and out. Each time that you slide it in, take a little bit more of his penis in until you have taken as much of it into your mouth as possible. Then start over again with just the head.
- Take his penis into your mouth, then hold your head and mouth still. Allow him to move his penis in and out in any motion that pleases him. You may need to use your hand to stabilize his penis at the base and control the depth of penetration to prevent gagging, but this is a great way to learn what kind of motion and speed he likes.
- As you become more comfortable with fellatio, you will be able to extend your lips as you move up and down his penis allowing you to take more of his penis in.
- Extend his pleasure by bringing him close to the brink of orgasm, then slowing your oral stimulation. Slow your rapid in-and-out motions to gentle licks and kisses, then build back up to more vigorous action. When he's just about to explode, slow down again. Repeat several times before allowing him to ejaculate. You can intensify this technique by placing a cock ring around the base of his penis at the beginning of fellatio. When you are ready to let him ejaculate, remove the ring.

Dr. Hil says:

There's a Secret to Swallowing Semen

While many men fantasize about women enthusiastically gulping their juices—thanks in part to explicit porn movies— some women find the taste or consistency of semen difficult to swallow. It's a tricky situation, because many men feel that if you swallow their semen, it's a sign that you accept them completely. And if you love your partner, you don't want to hurt his feelings by spitting after he ejaculates or running to the bathroom to brush and gargle. He may take that as a rejection of an important symbol of his masculinity. But if the idea really turns you off, then doing it is not going to make for a mutually pleasurable sexual experience. Fortunately, there are steps you can take to make everyone happy.

- *Always show enthusiasm when performing fellatio.* Let him know that you are enjoying it. That may mean moaning with pleasure—the way you would if you were eating a decadent, orgasmic dessert.
- *Allow him to ejaculate in your mouth.* When you notice signs that he is about to come—he begins to pump faster, his breathing gets faster, and you begin to feel the initial contractions at the base of his penis—push the back of your tongue up against the roof of your mouth, protecting the back of your throat and the sensitive taste buds. That way, when he ejaculates, the fluid will pool in the front of your

continued

mouth. While the penis is still in your mouth, slowly allow the semen to flow out of the side of your mouth and onto the back of your hand. Later you can discreetly wipe your hand on the sheets or a waiting towel. He will never know the difference. It'll be your juicy little secret.

11
. . . . .

The Pleasures of Intercourse

In the old days, sex was defined solely as intercourse: his penis, her vagina, the missionary position, period. But over time, as we became more open about sex and sexuality, we started to think of sex in terms of foreplay and afterplay, oral and anal sex, doggy style, spooning, standing, sitting, and myriad other variations. We've become more willing to explore.

In addition to becoming more open, women have become more sexually empowered over the past forty years or so. We've learned to expect great sex, and we've dropped any pretense of shyness about getting just that. But by emphasizing female orgasm as essential to satisfying sex, we've perhaps inadvertently crowned oral sex the king of sexual techniques at the expense of intercourse. Because while it may be difficult for women to experience orgasm through intercourse alone, most of us can have wonderful orgasms through cunnilingus. Talk to some women and you come away with the feeling that intercourse has been relegated to the position of sexual stepchild.

Sex is not just about orgasms; having an orgasm should not be the goal. Sex is about *pleasure,* and there is no one way to achieve pleasure. Every woman is capable of experiencing sexual satisfaction in different ways. To increase your pleasure, focus on the physical sensations that you are feeling while making love. Savor his scent, the feeling of his skin against yours, and the movement of energy from his body to yours and back again. Honor and embrace your own unique experience of sexual pleasure with or without orgasm.

In my opinion, intercourse has always been—and still is—an option that offers a great deal of sexual interest and variety, and can be as "effective" as oral sex at bringing pleasure to you and your partner. Not only can it be physically thrilling, but, performed well, it also creates emotional and psychological pleasure that can't be duplicated by any other sexual technique.

Myths and Misunderstandings

As well educated as we are about sex, we still have a lot of misconceptions about intercourse. For example, we think that intercourse is "natural"—that men and women innately know what to do—and that, perhaps, as human animals we have an inherent drive to copulate. But "instinctive" sex is not *great* sex; *great* intercourse requires study and practice. And truly sensational intercourse is an art that requires the refinement of technique, a sensitivity to your partner, the ability to communicate verbally and nonverbally, and the ability to lose yourself—mind, body, and soul—in the experience.

We also tend to think of intercourse as boring, standard-issue, and uninteresting sex. Lying down together and placing a penis into a vagina seems unimaginative to some folks—lazy, inhibited, even boring. But intercourse is—or should be—a launching pad for a whole host of sexual experiences and experimentations. Ultimate intercourse offers literally dozens of positions to try. It's a total-body experience that involves kissing, gazing into one another's eyes, talking and sharing, using your hands to touch and explore each other. There are all kinds of ways to get and give pleasure during intercourse. There's nothing basic about it.

We sometimes think that the male experience of intercourse is very different from the female experience. We imagine it to be almost solely physical for men and almost totally emotional for women. The truth is that the experience of intercourse is both physical *and* emotional for both men *and* women. But every person is different—with different needs, desires, trigger points—in ways that have nothing to do with gender. The key to ultimate intercourse is to throw away your assumptions and start to really explore the pleasures that this intimate, rewarding, and exciting form of sex can bring.

The Male Experience

Men love intercourse. Why wouldn't they? It's the one activity that is almost certain to end with their orgasm. In addition to the physical rewards of intercourse, men also describe a feeling of emotional closeness—a joining of spirits—that can't be duplicated in any other way. For some men, intercourse is the way that they show love for a partner and gain a sense of acceptance from her.

But intercourse can also be a source of stress for a man, too. He wants to appear strong and virile to you. He needs to be reasonably fit, since most sexual positions require strength and stamina, especially those in which the man is the most active participant and must support his own body weight. In order to perform sexually, he must obtain an erection and maintain it for a reasonable amount of time, ideally until he's brought you sufficient pleasure. He worries that his penis may not be long enough, thick enough, hard enough. He worries about hitting all of the right spots and whether he will last long enough to satisfy you. He's feeling responsible not only for his pleasure but also for yours. And the catch there is that he actually has little or no control over whether you'll be satisfied or not. These are the thoughts that may be bouncing around in his head even as he's trying to remember what kind of strokes you like. All this causes a certain level of performance anxiety for many men (and for *all* men at some point in their sexual lives).

If you care for him and want to develop a good sexual relationship, it's important that you try to lessen his performance anxiety by letting him know that great sex is not dependent on a huge or hard penis. (It's not, by the way.) And it's not about the goal of orgasm. It is about the pleasure that you two can share and exchange.

The Female Experience

For many women, if not most, intercourse is extremely intimate. During no other sexual act do you feel as close to your partner as you do during intercourse. It is the one activity in which you may come away feeling a strong bond, a sense of "oneness." That makes sense when you consider the fact that you are accepting this person *into* your body, your temple, your sacred space. Even a woman who tells herself she can have casual sex or a one-night stand may find herself becoming more emotionally attached to her partner than she imagined possible.

That emotional connection may be the main reason women favor intercourse. Unlike men, women are not guaranteed an orgasm during intercourse. In fact, as lovely as the experience may be, intercourse is not a very efficient way for a woman to obtain an orgasm. I didn't say you *can't* experience an orgasm through intercourse; I'm saying it's not the easiest way. More on that in a moment.

Intercourse is the one activity that women cannot be rushed into.

We need more time than men to reach sexual ecstasy as well as a lot more time to prepare for intercourse, both emotionally and physically. Emotionally we need to feel safe and secure—we want to trust the person we're about to let into our sacred space—and physically we need time to become aroused, wet, open, and ready for intercourse.

All this can make some women anxious. We worry that we won't be able to reach our orgasm or experience enough pleasure before our partner ejaculates. But if he doesn't come quickly, we worry that he doesn't find us sexy and desirable. In fact, many women spend more time worrying about their partner's pleasure than about their own. And some women become so preoccupied with their partner's experience that they don't focus on their own pleasurable sensations.

Fortunately, the sexual experience is not just about experiencing an orgasm. For many women, the intimacy and emotional pleasure that comes from having intercourse is satisfying enough. But in order to fully enjoy sex you need to be able to let go and concentrate on the sensations you're experiencing. You have to be an active participant. Sure, you could just lie back and be a receptacle for his penis, but for ultimate intercourse, you have to be into it, an equal partner in the sharing of bodies.

Ten Keys to Ultimate Intercourse

Good sex is an activity that physically pleases both you and your partner. Great sex involves connecting with one another—mentally and physically—even more intimately. Ultimate intercourse is a physical, mental, emotional, and spiritual pursuit that involves the entire body, all your senses, your voice, your mind, your very breath.

There are several basic principles to keep in mind when you are having sex that will help you have the best possible sexual experience, lovemaking so spectacular that it will make the actual physical act almost secondary.

1. Involvement

In the far recesses of our minds, some of us still believe that women should be the more passive participants in sex: It's not "ladylike" to be too eager; let the man make the first move. But intercourse is a shared pleasure, and women should be active participants. In fact, men are turned on by women who approach intercourse with enthusiasm, confidence, and attention.

You have to be totally involved in and focused on the pleasure you are giving as well as receiving. Don't just lie there and wait for him to do all the work; get in there and play, experiment, try new things to turn you both on. To experience the most pleasure, you have to lose yourself in what you're doing. Learn to tune out the noise and turn off mundane thoughts; focus only on your sexiest fantasies and the pleasurable physical sensations you're experiencing. It's okay to be selfish and go after your own pleasure. After all, your pleasure will increase his.

And approach sex with confidence. Wake up that sexy, sensual woman who lives inside you, the one who knows what she wants and how to get it as well as give it. Don't hide behind shyness and uncertainty. Get bold. Be seductive. Sex is fabulous. You know you enjoy it, so go for it.

2. Setting the Scene

We think of sex as being about what we feel—the warmth, the wetness, the softness of skin touching skin—but really fantastic sex comes from stimulating all the senses.

Sight

First make sure the room you're planning to make love in is warm and neat. Clutter can be a distraction. Besides, you want to have plenty of room to spread and roll around.

Light candles or drape a lamp with silk scarves to create a soft, romantic glow; use a red or blue bulb to create a mood; plug in a simple night-light. Just give yourself enough light so that you can see one another. Watching your partner's ecstasy can be a wonderful turn-on: when he sees you're excited, it'll arouse him even more, and the excitement will just build up. Stimulate his sense of sight by wearing something erotic: a bustier with thigh-high stockings, a silky bra with matching thong, a teddy made of something soft, or a nice pair of satin pajamas. Look into his eyes and strip for him, slowly removing your clothing one piece at a time while he watches. Don't worry if you don't look like a Victoria's Secret model. Believe me, he's much more focused on what you're doing—and what you're going to do to him—than on the size of your thighs.

Sound

Set the mood with music you both like. It can be slow and romantic or more upbeat, depending on the mood you want to set, but it shouldn't be too loud or distracting. What you really want to hear is your own erotic body sounds: your bodies moving together, your juices flowing, your moans of delight. Remember that the sound of your pleasure turns your partner on. (Ancient texts describe as arousing the hissing sound you create when you suck air through your teeth signaling your pleasure.) And don't be afraid to talk to your man; words of romance or your naughty thoughts whispered in his ear can add to his arousal.

Smell

In anticipation of a sexy, romantic encounter, fill your room with fragrance. Put a heady bouquet of flowers in a vase by your bed. Light scented candles, use an aromatherapy diffuser, or put a few drops of essential oil on a warm light bulb to infuse the room with sensual scent. (But keep it subtle, not overwhelming.) Add just a touch of fragrance to your body as well. You may want to relax in a perfumed bubble bath or apply a fruit-scented lotion. A secret: You don't even have to use exotic or expensive perfumes. I've read that men are turned on by familiar scents like vanilla or cinnamon. Why not dab a little vanilla extract behind your ears or along your thighs? Don't wear so much fragrance that it overwhelms your natural body scents. The "musk" and pheromones you release when you're aroused and the smells you create when your bodies come together, are sexier than anything you'll find in a bottle.

Taste

Make food part of your foreplay. Enjoy a simple, sensuous meal in bed. Talk and relax as you feed each other; it's a great way to get intimate before you get *intimate*. Or put a bowl of strawberries, melon balls, chocolate truffles, or other succulent snack by the bed to feed each other. You might also try using flavored lubes, chocolate sauce, honey, or jam to smear on each other, then suck and lick off. (Be careful to ensure that anything you place in the vagina is easily removed to prevent infections.) Or skip all of the above and focus on the taste of one another's bodies. Enjoy the saltiness of skin, taste the sweetness of lips, notice the complex and unique flavors of your secretions. Your lover is a smorgasbord; *bon appétit*!

Touch

Ultimately, it will always come back to touch. As you remember to keep your skin and your lips soft and smooth, don't forget your surroundings. Dress the bed in clean, comfortable sheets. Satin may be sexy, but it may be impractical; good-quality cotton is just as smooth and sensual. Have lots of pillows on hand to build a cozy love nest for you and your partner or to help you assume a variety of sexual positions.

3. Arousal

Intercourse should only begin when you both are maximally aroused, absolutely begging for it. But arousal, like all aspects of really great sex, takes time. It cannot be rushed. Though you may be thrilled at the very thought of having sex, enjoy the anticipation, which can be just as much fun (or more!) than the actual intercourse. Spend time exploring one another's bodies with your hands and your lips—kissing, caressing, massaging, touching—before you begin intercourse. Gaze into his eyes. Ask him if he likes what you're doing. Ask him what you should touch next. Really get to know his body; help him get to know yours.

As you become more aroused, your vagina becomes longer and wider at the top in preparation for receiving your partner; it also becomes wet. All that lubrication makes for great intercourse because it not only allows the penis to move in and out of your vagina more easily but also helps transmit messages of sexual stimulation to your nerve endings. If you're not properly lubricated, intercourse will cause friction, which is uncomfortable at best. It could even hurt you or your partner.

Don't judge your level of arousal by how wet you are, however. Every woman is different: some will produce copious amounts of lubricating fluids while another will produce very little no matter how aroused she is. Other factors: Your natural juices may lessen as you age. Medications like antihistamines and birth control pills may also affect lubrication. Even condoms can be drying. But don't worry; if you need to "supplement," use a water-based lubricant to replace natural moisture and help make sex more enjoyable. Make it a part of your foreplay. Rub it on his penis and ask him to rub your vulva and vaginal opening. Keep more nearby so you can apply it as you need it; lubes may dry up after prolonged intercourse and may need to be reapplied during sex.

4. Communication

For ultimate intercourse it is important to communicate what you want and to let him know he's doing it right. Start with what I call show-and-tell. Tell your partner about what, where, and how you want to be stimulated. Don't make it a criticism of what he's doing, and unless you're engaged in domination play, don't make demands. Whisper in his ear, gently describing what you want. Make it sexy. Then take his hand or his penis and guide it to the place that gives you the most pleasure. Place your hand gently over his hand, then move it at the speed and intensity that you desire. He'll quickly learn the tempo, the amount of pressure, and the kind of motions that unlock your passion.

The second part of communication is letting him know he's doing it the way you like it. Let him know when he hits the right spot. Tell him just how much pleasure he is giving you. When something feels especially good, say so; he has no way of knowing otherwise. There's no better way to encourage a man to do what you want him to do than to let him know he's doing a very good job at turning you on. Besides, men are turned on by the sights and sounds of a woman who is enjoying herself. Moan, groan, pant, call his name, but make sure he knows your groans are expressions of pleasure. He'll be grateful for the information.

5. Positions

If you've ever seen an illustrated Kama Sutra or Chinese pillow book, you know there are literally hundreds of possible positions for intercourse, some so complex and difficult that only a contortionist would attempt them. You don't have to go for acrobatics to have great sex, but you should explore a variety of sexual positions just to keep things fresh and interesting.

All positions are variations on six themes: man on top, woman on top, side to side, sitting, standing, and rear entry. We'll go into more detail on positions later in the book. Keep in mind that the positions you choose will depend on several factors:

Your body type and his. For instance, is there a large discrepancy in weight or height between you and your partner? How well do your bodies fit together? Positions can compensate for any mismatches in size.

The size of his penis. If he's on the small side, certain positions may not allow the friction, pressure, or depth of penetration you need. If he's large, some positions may create too much penetration and discomfort. But choosing the right position can give you just the level of penetration that pleases you both.

The strength of your pelvic floor. When your pelvic floor is weak, you have less support for your vagina. It may feel wider and make it more difficult to produce a lot of friction during sex. Fortunately, you can choose positions that increase the friction you and your partner feel. You can strengthen your pelvic floor muscles and make your vagina feel tighter by performing Kegel exercises every day. (See chapter 6 for a complete description of Kegel exercises.)

Your flexibility and strength. Some positions require more agility than others. Choose those that won't put undue strain on your muscles and joints. Pain rarely leads to pleasure (unless you enjoy S&M).

Your physical fitness and stamina. If you are both physically fit, you'll be able to sustain a variety of positions. But if one or both of you could use some physical conditioning, you'll want to choose your positions wisely, sticking to those that won't cause you to run out of steam before you reach the finish line.

Your sensitive spots. Every woman is different. Most will find that the clitoris is her most sensitive spot, the one most likely to lead to orgasm or to intense pleasure. For others, the front wall of the vagina (the G-spot), the cervix, fornix of the vagina, or even the back wall of the vagina are the trigger points. Choosing a position that stimulates these areas will produce the most pleasure.

The kind of "ride" you like. Do you desire slow, relaxing lovemaking or pounding, wild, no-holds-barred sex? The positions that you choose will determine how fast or slow or far you'll go.

Personal preference. Once you start to experiment with different positions, you and your partner will learn which positions provide both of you with pleasure. Those are the ones you'll practice again and again.

So try something new, something you've never done before. Worst case scenario: You tumble over in one another's arms, laughing at your attempts, but that will just add to the fun. More likely, you'll find some positions you like. Once you perfect a few new ones, learn how to move smoothly from one to the next during your sexual encounter. Also remember to vary the positions you use from one encounter to another. It will certainly add a spark to your sex life.

6. Movement

Once you've got the positions down, you will want to learn how to put them in motion. Movement is what truly separates good intercourse from ultimate intercourse. A woman who knows how to move her pelvis to meet her partner's thrust and to control the penetration and motion of his penis is a woman who will give her man an experience to remember. She'll also greatly increase the chance that she'll have a mind-altering sexual experience of her own.

But meeting his thrusts doesn't mean going at it wildly. Rapid thrusting does not necessarily result in better sex. Intercourse should begin with slow, rhythmic movements, enabling the two of you to get into a groove together, allowing your bodies to warm up and your excitement to build. Vary the speed and depth of penetration during sex; change the angle of penetration and thrusting.

I believe one of the best ways to learn erotic sexual movements is to take belly dancing or African dance classes. If you can find an erotic dance class or a class that teaches you how to strip, so much the better. These forms of dance teach you how to loosen up and get you in touch with your midsection, a part of the body that is vital to sexual movement. But if you can't find such classes in your area, practice some of my groove moves on your own.

7. Variations: Speed, Angles, and Depth

Intercourse can be fast or slow, deep or shallow. You can approach one another from the front, back, or side. And you'll want to try it all at one point or another, because variety will put the spice in your sex life.

It's best to begin your lovemaking with slow, probing movements, then vary the speed and depth of your pelvic movements as you go along, sometimes fast and strong, sometimes slow and gentle. Remember: Sometimes no movement is a movement in itself.

Also, vary the depth of penetration of the penis. In the rush to "get it in and get it off," we tend to rush in—all the way "in"—right away, often overlooking the pleasure of shallow penetration. Most women find that their lower vagina is very sensitive and easily stimulated by shallow strokes. The head of his penis—also a very sensitive area—can be massaged by shallow strokes, especially if you contract your PC muscle as he withdraws his penis. This is a great way to start off.

Groove Moves

Developing a repertoire of sexy moves takes practice. Try these moves standing up, perhaps as part of your regular exercise routine, then do them lying on your back and on your stomach. Keep practicing until you get the movements smooth and fluid, then try them with your partner. You'll both be glad you did. (See my book *What Your Mother Never Told You About S-e-x* for more complete descriptions of these groove moves.)

- *Pelvic tilt:* Pull your stomach in, contract your buttocks, and thrust your pelvis forward. Try not to move your whole torso, just the pelvis. Release and repeat.
- *Swaying hips:* Put your weight on your left leg and move the right hip out to the side; shift your weight to your right leg and move your left hip out.
- *Twisting hips:* Isolate the right buttock and swivel your hip forward, then return to center. Now isolate the left, move the left hip forward, and return. Repeat. This variation on the pelvic tilt will help move the penis to different areas of the vagina during sex.
- *Hip circles:* Make a square by moving your hips forward, to the right, back, to the left, and front again. As you practice, round out the "corners" until you're moving in a slow, fluid circle. Vary the size of the circles. This is the move that really drives men wild.
- *Figure eight:* Imagine a figure eight on the floor and trace it with your hips by isolating the right hip and moving it

continued

forward, to the right, back, and center. Then isolate the left hip and move it forward, to the left, back, and center. You can trace the "8" from side to side and from front to back. It's more difficult than it sounds, but with practice it will become your most effective sex move.

Deep penetration is good for women whose sensitive spot is around the cervix or at the top of the vagina. Going deep also feels great to him because it enables the cervix to massage the most sensitive parts of the penis: the frenulum and corona. But be careful; this often leads to a quick orgasm for him. To make it work for both of you, start with shallow penetration and allow yourself to become fully aroused. This lengthens the vagina, providing more room for the penis at the top. (If you don't, deep penetration can be uncomfortable for you.) It also makes it more likely that you'll experience orgasm even if he comes quickly.

Also vary the angle of entry and the direction of his thrusting to create new and pleasurable sensations. Your vagina may have a highly sensitive area—or several—that are unique to you. Varying the angle of entry ensures that you discover and stimulate all of your most sensitive areas during intercourse.

He should vary not only his angle of entry but also the way he moves once he's inside you. Some approaches include:

- *Thrusting:* The energetic back-and-forth motion of his pelvis that we most commonly associate with sex.
- *Rocking:* A subtle back-and-forth movement of the pelvis. It's more of a pelvic tilt, not an in-and-out movement.
- *Pressing:* After fully inserting his penis, he presses his pelvis

against yours, bringing himself in contact with your most sensitive areas. He remains still, maintaining the pressure for a second or two, then releases and presses again. While pressing, he can practice his Kegel exercises (see chapter 6 for a description of Kegel exercises). They will cause his penis to move inside the vagina in interesting ways.

∝ *Churning:* After fully inserting his penis, he presses his pelvis against you with a circular, grinding motion.

8. Extragenital Stimulation

Ultimate intercourse involves so much more than a penis in a vagina. The genitals are only a relatively small area of your body; you and your lover have dozens of square inches of skin to explore. Yes, I'm talking about stimulating the well-known erogenous zones: kissing the mouth, nuzzling and nibbling the neck, sucking and licking the breasts. But don't stop there. Running your fingers through a

The Countdown

Here's a mind-blowing move to try the next time you have intercourse. The person on top is in charge of this exercise. It works just as well whether that's you or him.

Slowly insert just the head of the penis in the vagina. Now, using only shallow penetration, move in and out for ten strokes. Then take one very deep stroke and hold and press the penis deeply for just a second or two. Now take nine shallow strokes and one deep one. Count down until you're taking one shallow stroke and one deep thrust. (Don't worry if you lose count. If you really get into this move, you probably will. That's the idea.)

lover's hair has always been considered romantic. Stroke his back with your nails.

Find out what feels good to him, then stroke, massage, pinch, rub, kiss, and caress him before, during, and after intercourse.

9. Breathing

The breath is very important to ultimate intercourse. Breathing correctly helps you to relax so that you are more open to receiving pleasure. But many women tend to hold their breath during sex, which increases stress and inhibits relaxation. Breathing enhances sexual pleasure.

To practice breathing properly, take slow, deep breaths through your nose, concentrating on filling your entire abdomen, not just your rib cage. (A good, deep breath should cause your belly to expand.) Now slowly breathe out, pushing all the air out of your lungs and collapsing your abdomen. Allow yourself to make sounds—*aaah*s or grunts or whatever comes out—as you exhale. Notice how your body begins to relax. Practice deep breathing until it becomes second nature. When you're deep breathing during sex, you can increase your sexual energy further by relaxing your pelvic floor muscles completely as you inhale, then squeezing them as you exhale.

10. Afterplay

Ultimate intercourse does not end with (usually his) orgasm. Keep that intimate connection going by continuing to embrace, kiss, and stroke one another even after thrusting has ended. Gaze into his eyes as you lie cuddled together. Whisper in his ear, telling him how much you enjoyed lovemaking. You may find yourselves laughing in sheer delight, or perhaps you'll find that it is a deeply tender time. Whatever the emotions that come after your lovemaking, don't rush to get dressed or let yourself fall asleep before you've taken the time to enjoy the moment.

Getting in Position for Pleasure

You only have to take a peek at a copy of the Kama Sutra to understand that sex is an activity of infinite variety. There are literally hundreds of possible "unions" or postures for lovemaking. If you're trying to add diversity and spark to your sex life, it's helpful to have a variety of positions in your repertoire.

In this section, we'll look at the six basic positions—man-on-top, woman-on-top, side-to-side, sitting, standing, and rear entry—and explore several variations on each of them. That makes for more than fifty options to explore, more than enough to keep you and your lover busy for months to come.

Man on Top

The so-called missionary position is the most common position for intercourse, and there's a reason for that. This position really promotes a sense of intimacy between partners, allowing you to gaze into each other's eyes, kiss and caress, and maintain total body contact throughout the experience. It's easy, feels natural, and is relatively comfortable for both lovers.

The Basics

You lie on your back with legs spread and knees slightly bent. He lies between your legs, facing you, and guides his penis into your vagina, supporting his body weight with his arms or elbows.

Your Pleasure

Missionary appeals to women who love the feeling of "being made love to." He's in control, so you can relax and enjoy the ride. If your movement is somewhat restricted, that doesn't mean you should be passive. From this position, you can kiss his lips, face, and shoulders; caress; and massage him. Grab his buttocks and pull him closer, deeper, and enjoy the feeling of a complete oneness.

It may be difficult for him to stimulate your clitoris from this position unless he takes special care to press his pelvis close to yours or you arch your pelvis up to meet him. You'll get more pleasure if you move your hips to meet his thrusts, or try one of the "Groove Moves" described earlier in this chapter. You can also stimulate your clitoris with your fingers as he thrusts.

His Pleasure

He controls the speed and depth of penetration and most of the pelvic movements, so he can make sure he experiences orgasm. (This is the easiest position for him to climax from.) He'll need to be sensitive to your needs as well. Fortunately, he can watch your expressions and whisper in your ear, so it's easy to communicate what feels good and what doesn't.

Note that this position can be tiring for him, especially if your lovemaking session runs long: He has to support his body weight while concentrating on moving his pelvis and making sure you're enjoying yourself. And it may be more of a problem for him if he's much heavier than you are.

Variations on the Theme

For each of these variations, start with the basic missionary position, then . . .

  Bring your legs close together and let his legs straddle yours. This will produce additional friction for you and your partner, and increase stimulation of your clitoris. This also decreases the depth of penetration, so it's ideal if he has a penis longer than the depth of your vagina. It's good if you have relaxed pelvic floor muscles or if his erection is not quite firm, because it tightens the vagina.

❧ He moves his right leg outside of your left leg, leaving his left leg between yours. If he doesn't have a very firm erection, this position enables him to use his inner thigh to support his penis as he thrusts. If you move your pelvis in a circular fashion—think of yourself as stirring something up—you may also increase stimulation of your clitoris.

❧ Put your straight legs on either side of his legs, allowing his pelvis to lie snuggly between them.

❧ Bend your knees and pull your thighs back toward your chest. (If you're still working on your flexibility, you can make this one easier by hooking your arms under both of your knees and holding and pulling your thighs back toward your chest.) This increases the depth of penetration, but the clitoris isn't stimulated. This is a good move if your sensitive spot is near your cervix or the fornix (top) of your vagina.

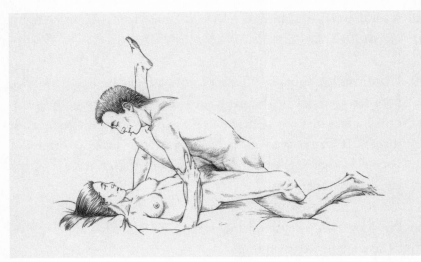

❧ Lift one leg up and, depending on your level of flexibility, let it rest against your chest, around his back, or over his shoulder while keeping the other leg straight. This changes the angle of penetration and enables him to stimulate a different area of the vagina. Add interest by switching the raised leg.

❧ Raise both legs and place one on each of his shoulders. This offers the deepest penetration to women who are very flexible.

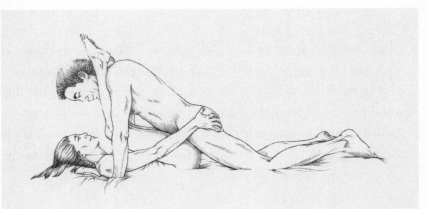

❧ Raise both legs and wrap them around his waist. Penetration will be deeper, and you'll also pull him closer to your clitoris.

❧ Place a pillow under your hips and keep your legs straight. This raises the clitoris and increases its contact with his penis.

❧ Raise your legs and, keeping them closed, place both of them on one of his shoulders. Keeping the legs closed increases friction.

❧ Raise one leg straight up, keeping the other one straight out, then lower the raised leg and swing the other one up. Just think "scissors." The movement of your legs constantly changes the angle of penetration and stimulates different parts of your vagina.

❧ Raise your pelvis up to meet his thrust and move your hips in a circle. Squeeze your PC muscle on the upswing.

❧ Straighten your legs. He carefully rotates 90 degrees, without pulling out, until his body is at a right angle to yours. This enables him to stimulate the side of your vagina as he thrusts.

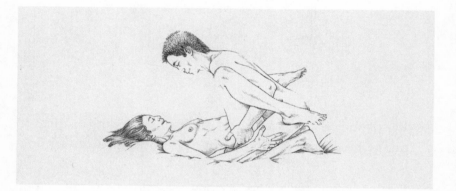

❧ Before he enters your vagina, he kneels and sits back on his ankles. You lie on the bed with your knees bent and feet flat. He elevates your buttocks and enters you. This position is visually stimulating, because you can each see so much more of the other's body and your hands are free to stimulate your clitoris.

❧ Before he enters you, he kneels. You lie flat with your legs pulled back against your chest or placed on his shoulders. He enters you and then leans back as far as he can. The pressure from his penis is directed at your G-spot.

❧ Lie on the bed and bring your pelvis to the edge. He kneels on the floor and enters your vagina as your thighs straddle his body.

📎 Lie on a table and bring your pelvis to the edge. He stands between your legs and enters your vagina. Raise both legs and place one on each of his shoulders.

📎 Relax your pelvis as he enters your vagina, letting him make all of the in-and-out movements. But as he's on an "out" movement, squeeze your PC muscle tightly. If he withdraws completely, you may hear a "snapping" sound. The pressure around the head of his penis will send him into orbit.

📎 Straighten your legs and, after he enters you, cross them at the ankles. This puts intense pressure on his penis.

📎 Pull your knees up and against your chest. He kneels, holds the base of his penis, and inserts it into your vagina. He moves the penis around in a circle inside the vagina.

Woman on Top

This position gives you the leading role, allowing you to control the speed of your movements and the depth and angle of penetration. Taking it from the top also gives you the orgasmic double whammy of deep penetration *and* stimulation of the clitoris in a way not possible in any other position.

Women often shy away from this position because they think it will expose too many of their physical imperfections. But men—visual creatures that they are—love having you on top where they can see and caress your body. And the position gives them a chance to lie back, relax, and enjoy the sensations. Believe me, they're not grading your appearance during this intimate time.

The Basics

He lies on his back. You kneel on the bed facing him and straddle his pelvis. Take his penis in your hand and guide it into your vagina. You can sit up or lie on top of him, supporting your weight with your arms or elbows.

Your Pleasure

If you don't like being in the passive role, here's where you can get more active. From this position, you have complete freedom of movement. Move up and down, press forward or lean back, sway, bounce, undulate, or try any combination of movements that will bring you pleasure. Because you control exactly how he enters you, you can ensure that all of your most sensitive spots are stroked or rubbed by his penis or pubic bone. Recent studies have shown that this position most stimulates the anterior wall of the vagina, or the G-spot. This is also a good position if you like stimulation of your cervix or fornix (the top) of your vagina.

Try woman-on-top positions if his penis is on the short side; they'll allow you to take advantage of the full length of his member.

But if he's bigger than average or your vagina is short, be careful; penetration may be too deep unless you modify the position.

His Pleasure

Men are turned on by seeing a woman's body and by being able to watch the pleasure on her face during lovemaking. This position allows him to get his fill of watching you, yet it keeps his hands free to roam your body, massage your breasts, stimulate your nipples and clitoris, and grab your buttocks. And because you're doing most of the work, he can concentrate on being pleasured.

If he tires easily or isn't feeling his best, this is a position from which he can still enjoy himself. This may also be a good position if he copes with premature ejaculation. Because it allows him to be more passive, his orgasm will be delayed, and his erection—and thus your lovemaking session—can last longer. On the other hand, some men find the position so visually stimulating that they experience orgasm faster.

Variations on the Theme

The woman-on-top positions can be done lying down, sitting up, or squatting, depending on your flexibility, strength, desired depth of penetration, and choice. Start by straddling him and then . . .

Lean forward, supporting your weight on your hands or elbows and straighten your legs, placing both of them between his legs. Penetration this way is shallow, but you get a lot of clitoral stimulation. This will work well for you when his erection is not quite strong.

Lean forward, supporting your weight on your hands or elbows and straighten your legs, placing both of them outside his legs.

⟡ Squat over his penis and ease it in. Then rotate your body and legs to the side of his body (right or left). The angle of penetration and stimulation is changed, hitting the side walls of the vagina and providing a different sensation for him as well.

⟡ From the sitting position, lean back, supporting your body by placing your hands behind you on the bed or by holding his hands. This increases stimulation of your G-spot, but it may be uncomfortable for him if his penis points up against his abdomen when he is erect.

⟡ From the sitting position lean back a bit, extending your legs forward so they're out in front of you (alongside his torso) but slightly bent. His legs should be straight but spread apart. You can put your hands on his knees behind you for stability. He can grab your ankles or feet to help maneuver your body back and forth during sex.

This time straddle him facing away from him before you gently
guide his penis into your vagina. Lean forward, supporting your
weight on your hands in front of you or on his thighs. Use your
thighs to raise yourself up and down. He can massage your anus
and buttocks while you caress his oft-neglected scrotum. If you're
flexible, you can lean farther forward and stabilize yourself by
holding his ankles. These positions may be uncomfortable for
him if his penis lies against his stomach when he's erect.

ℴ From the back-facing position above, you can lean back against his chest. (Have him sit up or recline on a stack of pillows.) Encourage him to massage your breasts or clitoris.

ℴ Place a pillow under his buttocks. This will push his pelvis up and forward and make it easier for you to grind your clitoris against his pubic bone.

ℴ Reach back and stroke his scrotum, perineum, and anus. Apply some lubricant to your fingers to increase his pleasure.

ℴ Try a number of pelvic movements: Begin with rocking movements; add side-to-side motions; move your pelvis in small circles, large circles, figure eights. By varying your movement, you increase the chance that your most sensitive spots will be stimulated. For him, the deep penetration and your movements, especially your circular motions, combine to create sensational pleasure for him as his penis is massaged by your cervix and fornix (roof) of your vagina.

ℴ Once you lower your vagina completely onto his penis, sit still for a few seconds, then use your PC muscle to squeeze his penis. Alternately, he can use his own PC muscle to flex his penis, moving it inside your vagina.

ℴ Before you let him enter you, take his penis in your hand and slowly move the head of his penis back and forth or in circles over your clitoris. You're using his penis like a paintbrush. Compliment the artistic abilities of his penis.

ᵒᐤ Relax your PC muscle as you slide onto his penis, then squeeze them tightly as you slowly lift yourself up.

ᵒᐤ Lean back slightly and place a battery-powered vibrator on your clitoris. Let the vibrations spread to your partner.

ᵒᐤ Slip a vibrating cock ring on his penis. Now sit upright on his penis and enjoy the shared vibrations. Lean forward to increase the pressure and intensity of the vibrations on your clitoris.

ᵒᐤ Lean forward, placing your body weight on his chest, then slide your bottom back until your clitoris is against the base of his penis. Now move your buttocks slowly from left to right, stroking your clitoris. This feels exquisite if you're one of the many women for whom the clitoris is most sensitive at three- and nine-o'clock positions.

ᵒᐤ Sit upright on his penis and use your hands to massage and stroke your breasts while he watches. Now reach down and stroke your clitoris the same way you do when you're masturbating.

Side by Side

This position is great for slow, romantic lovemaking. It provides the same benefits as the missionary position: good body contact and the ability to kiss, touch, and look at one another. But you also have more freedom of movement, and your hands are free to explore. This is a relaxing position that doesn't require a great deal of stamina from either of you; it's ideal if you're both tired.

The Basics

You both lie on your sides, facing each other. You can lift your top leg or wrap it around his waist to make it easier to insert his penis.

Your Pleasure

If side by side has one terrific benefit for you, it's that you can get good clitoral stimulation because this position enables you to get in close and press your pelvis against his. Depth of penetration is limited, so it's a good position if your vagina isn't deep or if he's very well endowed. You'll also enjoy the feeling of intimacy and sharing this position provides.

His Pleasure

This position gives him more control of his ejaculation so he can last longer—a plus for him and for you. He'll like the fact that his hands are free to roam, so he can touch you all over, including your clitoris and other erogenous zones. This position also gives him the best of both worlds psychologically: He doesn't have to give up control, but he doesn't have to be in charge either.

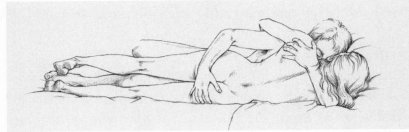

Variations on the Theme
Once you're in bed facing each other . . .

❧ Place your top leg over his top leg—along his thigh or around his waist—and the other in between his legs, interlocking your legs. This will give you great clitoral stimulation.

❧ Turn over on your back. He lies on his side, perpendicular to your pelvis (together your bodies look like a "T"), then raises both your legs, and enters from underneath. This way, the penis strokes the side walls of the vagina.

❧ Strap on a vibrating egg, then have him enter you from one of the positions above. You'll both be stimulated by the vibrations.

Rear Entry

Commonly referred to as the "doggy position," rear entry is a favorite of many couples. Both partners enjoy a good deal of freedom of movement, but he gets the most freedom here. He can stand up and hold on to your hips and buttocks or lean close to you and caress your breasts or kiss your back. Either way he's in perhaps the best position to really thrust his pelvis.

You benefit from this position if his penis is on the small side; there's nothing inhibiting his full entry. Many people assume that this is also a position that gives the best stimulation of your G-spot, but recent studies using MRI have shown that the posterior or back wall of the vagina gets the preferential stroking when you're entered from behind.

This position is also one in which the use of fantasy works well. If you want to play the bucking bronco, be spanked a little, or otherwise have him dominate, this is the position that suggests he's in control. Some people feel that this position doesn't allow as much intimacy since you're not facing each other. If that's a concern for you, it may help to compensate by placing a full-length mirror strategically such that you and your partner can see each other.

The Basics

You kneel on all fours, supporting yourself with your hands. He kneels behind you and enters your vagina from the rear. This can also be done while you're standing, supporting yourself on the edge of the bed or a chair, with him standing behind you. Likewise, he can enter you from behind as you lie on your stomach.

Your Pleasure

You're not going to get much clitoral stimulation in this position, but since his hands and yours are free, either of you can stimulate the clitoris manually. You can also squeeze your buttock muscles to increase pressure in your vagina and increase sexual tension and arousal. If you like to have your cervix or fornix (top of vagina) stimulated, this is a good position for you. His entry may be difficult if you are on the heavy side.

His Pleasure

This is one of the most popular positions among men (as evidenced by the number of times you see images in porn magazines of women ready to receive doggy-style sex). It's quite stimulating for the man who enjoys the sight of a woman's butt or likes watching his penis move in and out of the vagina. He gets to go deep and to direct his penis where he wants it to go, and his hands are free to stroke your buttocks, anus, breasts, and clitoris. Plus, this position gives him the greatest stimulation of the most sensitive part of the penis, the frenulum, which is massaged by your cervix when he penetrates you deeply. Whether because of the physical sensations or the excitement of being in such a "fantasy" position, his orgasm may come more quickly.

Variations on the Theme
You can try the rear-entry position kneeling, standing, or lying down.

🐾 Lie on your side, and have him lie down facing in the same direction, so that you're spooning. Lean forward slightly and arch your back to make it easier for him to insert his penis. Once he enters your vagina, press your thighs together to increase friction on his penis. Or lift your top leg for deeper penetration.

❧ Lie on your stomach with a firm pillow under your hips elevating your pelvis and buttocks. He lies on top of you and enters from the rear. Use your PC and buttock muscles to grip and massage his penis, or change the sensation by lying flat.

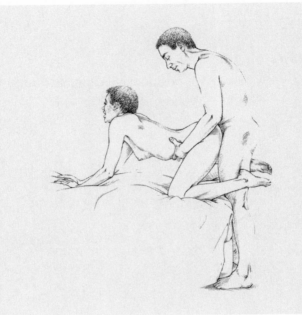

❧ Kneel on your hands and knees, then lower your head and chest down toward the bed, supporting yourself on your hands (think push-ups) or on your elbows. When he enters, this position presses the clitoris backward toward the penis and increases stimulation.

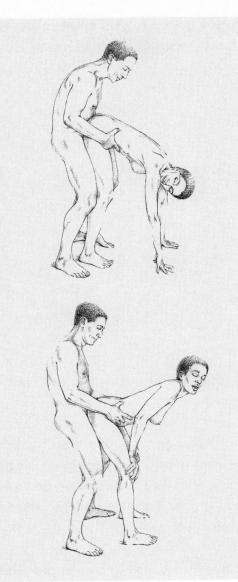

From a standing position, bend over, keeping your knees slightly bent, and place your palms on the floor. If you're not that flexible, put pillows on the floor or lean on the bed or a chair. As he enters you from behind, he should place his arm around your waist to help you both keep your balance. This variation allows him to hit your G-spot with better accuracy.

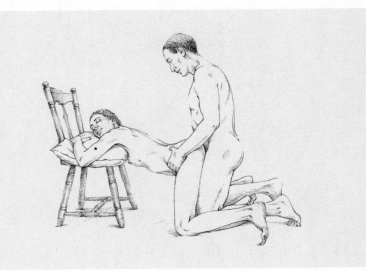

   Kneel on the floor and support your upper body on a chair. He kneels behind you and enters from the rear.

   Use the stairs: Kneel on the second step from the bottom (or third if your man is tall), and place your hands on the steps above you. Have him stand at the base of the staircase and enter you from behind. This position gets you out of the bedroom and will help mix things up.

   From a kneeling or standing position, let him enter you and begin thrusting, arousing himself thoroughly. Then ask him not to move. You take control of the action by moving your pelvis from side to side or back and forth on his penis. Let him watch you pleasure yourself.

Sitting

This is a very intimate position and a good one to start a love-making session. You can make eye contact, kiss and stroke one another all over, whisper sweet nothings, or nibble on his neck and ears. It's easy for either of you to reach your clitoris from this position, and if you like your nipples sucked, this posture puts them right in where he can get to them. He can penetrate you deeply, but his ability to thrust and move is limited. But that can be a good thing; his response may be a bit slower, so he may last longer.

The Basics

He sits on a chair or bed, with his feet in front of him or on the floor. You sit on his lap facing him, easing his penis into your vagina. Your feet can hang over the edge of the chair or wrap around his hips.

Your Pleasure

This is a winning position for you because it allows you both deep penetration and good stimulation of the clitoris. And since you're on top, you also control the angle and depth of penetration and the speed of your movements. Women tend to love the intimacy they feel in this position.

His Pleasure

What could be more relaxing for him than to be able to have sex sitting down? He'll enjoy being able to penetrate you deeply and to let his hands wander all over your body. And this position enables him to watch you in action and observe the pleasure he's giving you.

Variations on the Theme

    Have him sit on a bed with his legs spread in front of him. Facing him, wrap your legs around his waist or hips as you guide his penis into your vagina. Once he's entered, lean back and support yourself on your hands or elbows. This gives you both more leverage for thrusting.

🐚 Have him sit on a chair. You sit, facing away from him, lowering yourself onto his erect penis. If the chair doesn't have arms, you can spread your legs, making it easier for him to reach around and stimulate your clitoris. You can also reach down and stimulate the base of his penis.

🐚 Have him sit on a chair. You sit, facing him, lowering yourself onto his erect penis. Penetration is very deep.

ক্ষ He sits on a chair. You begin as above by sitting and facing him, then swing one leg over and to the side. The side walls of your vagina will be stimulated.

ক্ষ Have him sit with his legs loosely crossed "Indian style." Lower yourself onto his erect penis and wrap both legs around his hips. Lift one leg and then the other to vary the sensations in your vagina.

ক্ষ Use the sitting position as foreplay. Have him sit in bed with his legs straight and slightly parted. Then you sit on top with your legs either straight or wrapped around his back, *but don't let him enter you yet.* This is an arousing position because you can fondle each other's genitals and even rub them together without actual penetration. When you both become aroused, insert his penis, *but don't move.* Just sit still for a while with his penis inside you, squeezing your PC muscle just enough to keep him erect. (See page 52 for more information on your PC muscle.) He can also squeeze his PC muscle so you can feel him moving inside you. When you're both thoroughly hot and bothered, begin pelvic movements in this position or transition to another as you continue lovemaking.

Standing

You can have lots of exciting foreplay standing up; when one of you pins the other against a wall, kissing, groping and tearing at clothes, it suggests desire so strong you don't have time to get to the bedroom. But if you want to have actual *intercourse* this way, it will probably take some practice. First off, insertion may be difficult and depth of penetration can be decreased, especially if either of you is much taller than the other. To compensate, the shorter partner can stand on a stool or other object (find something sturdy and stable so you don't tumble over as you get into the heat of the action). You may also find that it's difficult to thrust while you're trying to keep your balance in this intertwined position. It also requires physical strength and stamina, because, in some variations, he's literally holding you up. If you can manage all this, it's a very exciting position that enables you to enjoy good body contact and to kiss, caress, and massage each other.

The Basics

Stand facing each other. If he's taller, he'll need to bend his knees and squat slightly so he can enter your vagina with an upward motion. You can raise one leg to make it easier to insert his penis.

Your Pleasure

This is a fantasy position, so just the idea of doing it standing up is a turn-on. You'll also enjoy great clitoral stimulation, so your chances of experiencing an orgasm are increased.

His Pleasure

He probably won't be able to penetrate you deeply, but he'll enjoy the additional friction on his penis that this position allows. If he's able to lift you and thrust deeply, he'll feel powerful and strong. But you should both be careful; his penis can be damaged if you fall or move too abruptly in this position.

Variations on the Theme

Start with your legs slightly apart to give yourself more stability. You might also want to lean on or near a wall for extra support.

- ❧ Have him stand with his legs slightly apart. Stand close to him and, as he enters, lift one leg, wrapping it around his thigh or, if you're flexible, his waist. Or let him hold your thigh for support.

- ❧ Stand facing the wall and brace yourself against it with your hands. Arch your back and push your pelvis back and up. He can stoop slightly to enter your vagina from behind, holding your hips or wrapping his arm around your waist for stability. This variation allows him to fondle your breasts or stimulate your clitoris.

⚮ Sit on a table or desk and spread your legs. Let him stand in front of you, lift your legs slightly, and enter your vagina. You can support your body by propping yourself up with your hands behind you or by leaning back on your elbows. (This variation eliminates all the potential drawbacks of the standing position.)

Have him lean with his back against a wall. Facing him, have him lift you in his arms, holding you up by your behind with his hands interlaced and locked. Place your arms around his neck for added stability and either wrap your legs around his torso or place your feet flat against the wall behind him. You'll be more in control of the movements, either rocking your pelvis back and forth or extending your legs and pushing out from the wall for leverage. This challenging position works best for a man with good upper-body strength.

In a variation of the position above, have him lift you in his arms and press *your* back against the wall. You wrap your legs around his back and your arms around his neck. Your movement is restricted, but he has good leverage with which to thrust.

Partner Sex Woes

Sex is a shared activity, and the anatomy or sexual technique of your partner can affect your pleasure. Knowing how to adjust, compromise, and otherwise go with the flow can make the difference between sexual frustration and satisfaction. Below are some of the most common partner complaints of women who have attended my sex seminars.

He Comes Too Quickly

For some couples, sex begins with his erection and ends with his ejaculation. When his ejaculation occurs quickly, it may be difficult for you to achieve the ultimate level of physical pleasure. You may be left staring at the ceiling, feeling unsatisfied, frustrated, and even resentful.

Some men come quickly out of habit. The fear of being discovered while masturbating causes some men to rush to the finish line. If his penis is very sensitive, he may also need minimal stimulation to experience orgasm. Anxiety and relationship problems may also contribute to rapid ejaculations.

How long should a man last during sex? The answer to that question is unclear and irrelevant. The fact is, you are not being satisfied, so there is a problem. What to do? Begin by taking the emphasis off intercourse. Cunnilingus and manual stimulation of your genitals prior to intercourse may give you the opportunity to experience the pleasure that you deserve prior to, or in lieu of, intercourse. Adding a thick condom to your sex play may decrease the sensitivity of his penis and allow him to last longer. Creams designed to make a man last longer usually con-

℞ *continued*

tain a local anesthetic to decrease the sensitivity of his penis. But beware: these same creams may rub off on your clitoris and vagina, making them numb and interfering with your pleasure. Choose positions for intercourse that limit the depth of penetration, and give you more control, like the woman-on-top or side-to-side positions. Avoid the man-on-top position as it is the most stimulating for most men. Limiting your pelvic movements during intercourse may also help him last longer.

Have a heart-to-heart conversation with your partner about your concern. Chances are, he feels as bad as you do. A visit to a physician or sex therapist may be just what he needs.

He Takes Too Long to Come

Men, like women, are all different. While the average man will reach orgasm after three to five minutes, and some will ejaculate within seconds of sexual stimulation, others require thirty minutes or more. Women generally take longer than men to reach orgasm, and many women dream of a man who can hang in there until they are satisfied. But there are limits to each woman's endurance.

Some men, concerned about pleasing their female partners, have perfected methods to delay their ejaculation. And it is possible that he is actually trying to give you the prolonged stimulation that he thinks you need to be sexually satisfied. He may be relieved to hear that it is not necessary for him to thrust for such long periods of time.

It is also possible that he has a condition called delayed ejaculation that makes it difficult for him to reach orgasm during sex with a partner. There may be physical as well as psycholog-

continued

ical reasons for this problem. Men who have grown up in a home where sex was considered sinful or bad, as well as those who fear pregnancy or sexually transmitted infections, may find it difficult to let go during sex. Men who use strong, fast and furious strokes during masturbation may find the slower and softer pace of intercourse to be inadequate for a rapid orgasm. Medical problems like diabetes, high blood pressure, alcohol abuse, and medications such as antidepressants may all interfere with his ability to climax.

You are not doing anything wrong and should not doubt your sexual adequacy or technique. You and your partner may simply have different sexual rhythms. Sit down and talk to your partner about your concerns. Let him know that, though you enjoy sex with him, you are finding it difficult to participate in prolonged intercourse without pain and soreness. Find other ways, like oral sex, manual stimulation, or vibrators, to bring him close to orgasm prior to beginning intercourse. Use lots of water-based lubricants during intercourse to prevent your vagina from becoming dry and sore. Choose positions that give him more stimulation, like man-on-top. A visit to his physician is also advisable.

He Is Too Quiet During Sex

Great sex involves stimulating all of the senses—touch, sight, taste, smell, and hearing. Touch is easy—you can't even have sex unless you're touching your partner. You're probably going to kiss, tasting the subtle salt of skin and the sweetness of lips. And you may sometimes cloud yourself in fragrance and wear a filmy negligee so your partner can delight in your sexy gar-

continued

ments (before he takes them off to enjoy the sight of your bare skin). And you may moan and gasp and sigh, signaling to your partner that you are in ecstasy.

Hearing those sex sounds can be a powerful aphrodisiac. When your partner groans or breathes heavily, he's letting you know he's enjoying himself. When he's silent, you may wonder whether he is lost in pleasure or is simply bored.

Despite the noisy panting, grunting, and oh-oh-ooohing you hear during the sex scenes of your typical porno movie, many people—both men and women—are silent lovers. Why? One theory is that people learn to be silent for fear of being discovered while masturbating or while having illicit sex. That fear may cause them to develop a silent sexual style that continues into adulthood. For some men, there's also the fear that, in the throes of sexual climax, they may squeak, scream, or make some other noise that sounds less than virile. They keep silent to avoid that embarrassment. In other cases, the guy is being quiet so he can listen to *you*.

If you want him to be a little more openmouthed, set a good example by making your own sexy sounds—moan, groan, sigh, scream. Hearing some subtle sounds from you may encourage him to loosen up, let go of some of his inhibitions and let you hear his passion. But don't overdo it or he may feel like you're faking it. If that hint doesn't work, speak up outside the bedroom. Ask him why he's so quiet when you're making love. Some men find that concentrating on making noise is distracting and decreases their pleasure. Your partner may not even realize he's being silent. Or perhaps he's keeping mum for fear of turning you off. Find out what's holding him back and lovingly encour-

continued

age him to be more vocal in bed. Also remember that there are other signs that he's receiving pleasure: a strong erection, heavy breathing, perspiration, and hips that move with enthusiasm.

He Is Too Noisy During Sex

But what if you've got the opposite problem—not a silent lover, but one who sounds like a roaring freight train? That can be annoying and distracting—not to mention disturbing to the neighbors.

You'll have to handle this one with some finesse, because asking him outright not to be so noisy may make him self-conscious and interfere with his enjoyment of sex. On the other hand, he may not be aware of just how his voice level escalates when he's in the throes of lovemaking. Try this: Record your lovemaking session and play it back to him so he can hear it for himself. He may be surprised at how loud he is. (But beware: The sound of your lovemaking may just turn you both on instead. If so, you'll have to find another method of throwing him a hint!)

Rather than dampen his enthusiasm, perhaps it's best to take steps to make the noise less noticeable. Stuff towels under the door, cover the floor with rugs, and close the windows. Turn on some mood music or buy a white noise machine (like those used in psychiatrists' offices), or a machine that makes nature sounds to cover some of the sexy sounds. Worse comes to worst, you can always invest in some earplugs. (He'll definitely get the message then.)

And if you can't beat 'em, you can always join in the fun. Release your inhibitions and make some loud, sexy noises of your own. According to some ancient philosophies, making

continued

sounds during sex helps energy flow and increases your pleasure. Just make sure you've got understanding neighbors.

He Can't Find My Clitoris

Many of my patients complain that their lovers haven't been able to discover their clitoris. My response? Show him the way! To help him on his journey, you can always copy the illustration of the vulva in chapter 2 of this book, place a red arrow next to the clitoris, and tape it above your bed. But if you want to be a bit more subtle, try making a game of "show and tell" as part of your foreplay. Show him your most sensitive areas and demonstrate how you masturbate. Take his hand and place it on your clitoris, then put your hand on top of his and guide his strokes so that he knows the pressure, speed, and type of touch that turns you on.

If you want him to be able to hit the spot during oral sex, try the same technique—guiding his head and mouth to the proper place and, moving your hips, bringing his mouth into contact with your clitoris. One woman told me that she taught her lover how to give oral sex by comparing it with kissing. She had him lie back with his lips slightly parted, then, bringing her mouth perpendicular to his, she kissed his mouth the way she wanted him to kiss her vagina. He couldn't wait to try out that technique. It was a lesson he never forgot—much to both their delight.

Increase Your Pleasure

It is easy for intercourse to become routine and boring. We often follow the same routine with the same outcome. Plain old "vanilla" sex won't feel so vanilla if you add a bit of spice. A little more attention to detail and a little more willingness to experiment and have fun can make "regular" intercourse something you'll want to do, well, regularly. Here are some of the most important things a woman can do to increase her pleasure during intercourse.

Practice Mental and Physical Foreplay

Delay intercourse until you're very aroused and close to orgasm. You can start your juices flowing early by, say, calling your partner at work and telling him what you are planning to do with him later. Once you're home, continue to exchange sexy banter and innuendo while you're making dinner or even washing the dishes together. Then once you're in bed, kiss, lick, touch, tease, play, touch again, kiss some more. The build-up will make you both feel like you're going to explode.

Concentrate totally on your erotic sensations. Forget about having an orgasm; just focus on the moment and the pleasure you're feeling.

Indulge in your wildest fantasy. Fantasy increases arousal and keeps your mind focused on sex. Your mind certainly won't wander if you're imagining a romantic escapade with a handsome prince or your favorite movie star.

Stimulate Your Clitoris

Either of you can stroke your clitoris while you're having sex. It's easiest to do manually when you're on top, when the two of you are lying side to side, or when he's entered you from behind. You can just reach down and twiddle, tickle, massage, and stroke your clit and never stop thrusting. It feels wonderful. As always, focus on what feels good, and don't think of clitoral stimulation as simply a way to increase your chances of having an orgasm. Let go of the pressure and explore.

- In the man-on-top, woman-on-top, or on-your-side positions, close your legs after he inserts his penis. Not only will this allow his penis better contact with and stimulation of your clitoris, it also will shorten and narrow your vagina, providing extra pressure and friction on his penis.

- You get on top and, after he inserts his penis, lower your chest and place your full body weight on him. Press your pelvis back until your clitoris is pressed against the base of his penis. He should stay still and let you begin the in-and-out motion. On the upstroke, move your pelvis back and up, then move forward, then down and repeat. You're actually making a circle with your pelvis while you're stroking your clitoris against his penis. You can also reverse the circle by pressing against the base of the penis with the downward motion, then forward, up, back, and then down again against the base of the penis.

- Man-on-top (coital alignment technique): From the missionary position (he's on top this time), he should slide his pelvis forward toward you so that the base of his penis presses against your clitoris and his pelvis rides high on yours. Then instead of moving in and out, you and he should take turns leading each other in a rocking motion. Begin the upward stroke by moving your pelvis up and forward. He then takes over the downward stroke by moving his pelvis down, pushing your pelvis down and backward. Keep rocking back and forth at a steady pace. You can increase the stimulation of your clitoris by pressing it against his penis.

꙯ From the missionary position, place a firm pillow under your lower back. This will shift your pelvis and bring your clitoris more in line with the path of his penis. For even more stimulation while he's thrusting, keep your legs straight.

Work That PC Muscle

Intercourse is the activity that enables you to really put those strong, agile pelvic muscles to use. A strong PC muscle will enable you to squeeze, massage, and pull his penis during the union, giving him incredible pleasure. But these muscles also help you control where the penis goes, which increases the chance that your most sensitive spots are stroked. So you're ensuring your own pleasure as well. It's a win for both of you.

Practice Kegel exercises daily (*see chapter 6*). They'll strengthen your PC muscle, which you can then use to increase your chances of experiencing an orgasm and to make your orgasms more intense. And the best thing about them is that you can do them anywhere.

Squeeze your strengthened PC muscle during intercourse. Kegeling will increase blood flow to your genitals, increase sexual tension, and improve your concentration and focus on sex.

As you explore the many possibilities of intercourse, never forget the goal of ultimate sex: intense, deep, and intimate pleasure that you both experience together.

12
. . . . .

Anal Pleasures

Do you want to break one of the last remaining sexual taboos? You may be interested in trying anal sex. In my experience, it's probably the sexual practice that men and women are most curious about but have never tried. It's one of those topics that are just not discussed, and few sex manuals even mention it as an option. So, although there is a lot of curiosity about it, myths and misconceptions about anal sex abound. For example, we tend to think . . .

ꙮ *It's painful.* Not if you use proper technique. In fact, because the anus is surrounded by many nerve endings, when that area is stimulated it can be quite pleasurable. If you're feeling pain, something is wrong.

ꙮ *I'll get hurt.* Yes, you can injure your anus if you don't follow the safety rules for anal sex. (The same can be said for vaginal sex if you use poor and careless technique.) You have to be careful; make sure you're having fun safely.

Anal sex is a very intimate act. You're allowing someone to enter the "forbidden zone" of your body, and perhaps it's precisely the forbidden nature of anal sex that makes it erotic. It requires a certain level of trust, because you are placing yourself in a vulnerable position with your partner. For these reasons, the practice is commonly reserved for sharing with someone you really care about and with whom you have an emotional connection. For most women, anal sex is an acquired taste; others never learn to love it.

If you can get past some of your misconceptions about anal sex and open your mind to it, you might find that it's another perfectly viable option for adding interest to your sex life. I believe there are four keys to making anal sex more pleasurable: education, preparation, communication, and technique.

Education

To receive anal pleasure, you and your partner both have to understand the anatomy of the anus and rectum. The anus is a short tube—about an inch and a half long—at the end of your intestinal system. Sensitized by hundreds of nerve endings, it's encircled by two rings of muscle, the internal and external sphincters, which tighten to keep the anus closed and relax to release bowel contents.

You control the external sphincter, meaning that you can tighten or relax it at will. The internal sphincter, however, is another story. Because this muscle automatically tightens whenever you attempt to push something into your anus, you may not have comfortable anal sex even when you're very aroused and desire the penetration. In order to have enjoyable anal intercourse, you have to condition this muscle to relax. If you're patient, the muscle will get fatigued and make it possible to penetrate the anus completely.

The rectum is a 5-inch-long tube that connects at the top of the anus and makes several turns along its course inside your body. It doesn't contain many nerves, but some people like the feeling of fullness you get when a finger, toy, or penis enters the anus. And because the rectum is separated from the vagina by only a thin layer of tissue, some women find that it's possible to stimulate their G-spot during anal sex.

Preparation

Judging by the average porn video, anal sex is as easy as vaginal intercourse and within seconds of penetration you'll be swooning in orgasmic ecstasy. Needless to say, porn videos aren't all that realistic. In reality, you need to take some steps to prepare for pleasurable anal sex.

Let's start with your attitude: More than with any other sexual activity, it is important that you are both physically and mentally relaxed. With vaginal sex, even if you're totally disinterested, you can add some saliva or lubricant and go with the flow. Anal sex works best if you really want it and are able to be totally present with your partner. Sure you can do it just because he begs you to, but chances are *his* eagerness won't make *you* enjoy it any better. In fact, unless you're into it, it can actually be painful. It can hurt, too, if you are anxious or convinced that it is going to be painful, because your anal muscles just won't relax.

You've got to lube up! I can't emphasize lubrication enough. Unlike your vagina, your anus and rectum don't produce their own lubrication, so in order to have painless intercourse in the anus, you have to use lots of lubricant in your anus and on his penis. Choose a silicone-based lube that's long lasting and water soluble, like Eros Bodyglide,

Wet Platinum, or Maximus. Avoid flavored, scented, and warming lubes; they may cause irritation. And never use oil-based lubricants like petroleum jelly or vegetable oil, which can clog the glands in your anus and cause an infection or cause your condom to break.

Yes, you should use a condom. Here's why:

- Anal intercourse is the easiest way to transmit HIV and other sexually transmitted infections. Using a condom decreases the risk.
- Men who penetrate the anus without a condom increase their chances of getting a urinary tract infection.
- It allows you to relax without concern about the contents of your anus and rectum. Everyone stays clean and infection free.

Choose a lubricated latex or plastic (polyurethane) condom, but avoid the ones with nonoxynol-9 or other spermicides, which may irritate the delicate tissue in the anus or rectum. And keep a few nearby when you're going to be participating in different kinds of sex during your lovemaking session. You'll need to change condoms each time you move from anal sex to vaginal intercourse; otherwise you could get a vaginal infection.

One thing you *don't* have to be concerned about is the contents of your rectum—"spills," so to speak. The anus and rectum are usually free of feces. It's definitely not a good idea to give yourself an enema just before anal sex. This may create tiny tears in the delicate tissue, increasing your risk of contracting HIV or other sexually transmitted infections. In addition, you may not expel all of the contents prior to sex and make matters worse.

Communication

Once you've decided that you both want to try anal intercourse, it's imperative that you and your partner approach it as a team and communicate throughout the process. As the recipient of anal sex, you should get to set the pace, letting your partner know when he needs to slow down, speed up, or stop completely. Pain is a definite stop sign, an indication that something is wrong. Tell your partner immediately if, at any point, you feel pain. Do *not* just grit your teeth and bear it; doing so may result in tears or other injury to your anus and rectum. Stop what you're doing, wait, and start again later if you wish. If you are enjoying what he is doing, let him know that as well.

Getting Started: Anal Sex 101

The most common mistake that couples make when they decide to try anal sex is to proceed without proper preparation. The result is usually pain. Failure to prepare properly can not only cause you a lot of discomfort but, if the first time is painful, it's likely that your muscles will never fully relax and subsequent attempts will also be painful as well.

Following the "desensitizing" steps outlined below* will increase your chances for pleasure the first time—and the next and the next. It takes several days to work up to actual penetration, but think of it as extended foreplay. It's worth the wait.

Day 1: Begin with a warm bath. Your partner should kiss, stroke, and massage your body to help you relax. When he reaches your buttocks, he should massage, stroke, and knead these muscles until they relax, then gradually move his fingers to the space between your butt cheeks and allow his fingers to lightly pass over your anus.

*NOTE: For all of these steps, his fingernails should be trimmed short and be free of sharp edges to avoid injury.

Day 2: Repeat the steps from Day 1. Allow the massage to evolve into oral or manual stimulation of the clitoris and vagina. As you become more aroused, he should apply a generous amount of water-based lubricant to his index finger and begin to gently massage your anus. He should start with long, slow strokes, then move his finger in circles around the opening. Breathe deeply and concentrate on the pleasure you feel when this sensitive area of your body is touched.

Day 3: Repeat Days 1 and 2. After at least ten minutes of anal massage, he should begin to gently push his well-lubed finger against the opening to your anus with steady pressure. Breathe deeply. As you inhale, contract your pelvic-floor and anal muscles; as you exhale, relax these muscles. Each time you exhale, he should increase the pressure against the anus, then hold his finger still until the next exhale. Then more pressure, then hold. *Note: many couples feel more comfortable using a protective finger cot, condom, or latex gloves to cover the fingers during manual anal sex play.*

Day 4: Repeat Day 3, but this time let him continue pressing his finger against the opening of your anus until he has inserted it an inch or two. Breathe and focus on staying relaxed. When you're ready, let him move his finger around in small circles. Eventually, he can begin to slowly move his finger in and out, simulating intercourse. It helps to continue to stimulate your clitoris, orally, manually, or with a vibrator. And make sure that you are using lots of lube and reapplying as necessary.

Day 5: Warm up with the steps described above. This time, lubricate a small dildo or butt plug (find one no larger than ⅝ inch in diameter) and, as you breathe deeply and relax, have him slowly insert it. As the toy passes your internal sphincter, you may get the sensation that you need to move your bowels. This is normal; try to ignore it. Definitely resist the urge to tighten your muscles. Hold the dildo still for a few minutes and let your body get used to it. Then let him begin slow, shallow movements in and out. (See chapter 15 for more about anal toys.)

Day 6: After you've warmed up sufficiently, it's time to include his penis in your anal play. Lie on your side and have him lie behind you. Before any anal contact is made, put the condom on him and lubricate his penis and the opening to your anus well. (If you've done the manual stimulation above, the inside of your anus should be well lubricated as well. The more lube, the better.) Bend forward slightly to make your anus easier to reach, and begin by rubbing his penis along the outside of your anus. (Because of all the nerve endings in this area, you may find this to be quite pleasurable.) Place his penis at the opening and ask him to press against it gently as he did with his finger on Day 3—with firm, steady but gentle pressure. When you feel ready, you can begin to push your anus back onto his erect penis. (If you do the pushing, you can remain in control of the action.) If you feel resistance or some slight discomfort, stop moving and just maintain the pressure until the feeling subsides. Tell him to keep his penis still until your muscles relax and you're ready to proceed with deeper penetration. Breathe deeply; on the exhale, push farther back against his penis. Continue pushing, resting, pushing, and resting until the head of his penis has entered your anus. (You may not be able to fully insert the penis the first time. That's okay. Be patient.)

When he's penetrated you, again, ask your partner not to move. You should now squeeze your pelvic-floor and anal muscles and then relax them completely. If you like, you can push farther back each time you relax your muscles. At this point, he'll probably have a strong urge to start thrusting. Remind him to control the urge, or he may never have an opportunity to get near your anus again. Forceful insertion can tear your anus and cause a fissure.

You and your partner can decide at this point which of you will lead. Either you can continue to move against his stationary penis, or he can begin an in-and-out or circular motion. Small movements are all that either of you will need. Wild, deeply penetrating thrusts are more likely to cause discomfort and a very sore if not injured rump. Work together to find the stroke and rhythm that works best for both of you. If at any time you feel that your anus is becoming dry, add more lubricant. Have him pull out slowly, apply more lube, then enter gently and carefully again.

More Positions for Anal Intercourse

Once you've gone through the steps above and gotten your body and mind conditioned to receive anal sex, you can try some of these alternate positions.

- He lies on his back. You straddle him, facing him, and lower yourself onto his penis. This position gives you control of the initial insertion of the penis as well as the depth of penetration, speed, and rhythm of intercourse.
- You lie on your stomach. Place a pillow under your pelvis to lift your buttocks. He lies on top of you with his pelvis against your butt. This position allows you or your partner to stimulate your clitoris while you're enjoying anal sex. You might also place a wandlike vibrator underneath your pelvis to add intensity.
- You lie on your back with your legs pulled back against your chest or resting on his shoulders. He kneels and enters from above.
- You kneel on hands and knees, doggy style. He kneels behind you, keeping his back up and holding on to your hips, and enters from behind. This position allows the deepest penetration and gives your partner the most control.

You should *not* have anal intercourse if:

- You have bleeding from your anus or rectum.
- You have an anal fissure.
- You have very large or bleeding hemorrhoids.
- You are pregnant.
- You had a heart attack within the past four weeks. (Discuss with your doctor first.)
- You are taking medications to thin your blood (anticoagulants).
- You have inflammatory bowel disease.
- You have a bowel infection.

More Anal Sex Play

Self-pleasuring

If you enjoy the sensations of anal sex play, it's easy to incorporate it into your private self-pleasuring routine. The best way to begin exploring the possibilities is in the shower. Using a hypoallergenic cleaning bar, soap up your fingers and massage the area surrounding the opening to your anus. You can also use a long-lasting, waterproof lubricant like Eros Bodyglide. Slowly insert your finger as described above.

You can also use a toy designed specifically for anal sex play. (See chapter 15 for more about anal toys.) These are smooth, free of sharp edges, and no more than 5 inches long. Most are tapered—thinner at the top than the bottom—so the anus gradually dilates when you insert the toy. They also have a flared base to prevent complete insertion of the toy. Unlike the vagina, your rectum is not closed at the top, and objects can be sucked inside. Every emergency-room physician has stories about the strange objects he or she has removed from someone's anus. You don't want to be coffee-break conversation.

Some women love the full feeling of having an anal toy inside them while they stimulate their clitoris or vagina. The muscles that are stretched by the toy are the same ones that contract during orgasm, so orgasms you experience this way may be more intense.

Stimulating His *G-spot*

Men who are able to relax and allow you to explore their anus may experience extreme pleasure from anal sex play. Many men, however, resist anal exploration because of the myth that only homosexuals enjoy being on the receiving end of anal sex. If he'd get over the myth, he'd figure out that men also have a G-spot that, when stimulated, may drive him wild.

He should lie on his back with his knees bent, while you kneel between his legs. Use lots of lube and massage his anus. Following the steps already described above, slowly enter his anus with your finger while you massage or lick his scrotum, penis, and inner thighs at the same time. As you stroke, move your fingers as if beckoning someone to "come here." When your finger is all the way in, begin a slow massage of the front wall of his rectum (the side nearest his penis). You'll feel a small bulge. That's the prostate gland; stroking it can provide some men with indescribable pleasure. Just below the prostate gland is a small dimple that has been described as the male "sacred spot" in some ancient texts and may be even more sensitive than the prostate gland. Each man is different, so try stimulating both areas. The combination of fellatio or a hand job with anal pleasuring may be a mind-altering experience for him.

Anal Fisting

- In anal fisting, your partner's entire hand is placed in your rectum. If you want to try it, be sure to follow the rules below. And be aware that frequent overstretching of your anal sphincters may cause them to lose some of their tone, which can lead to bowel- and gas-control problems.
- Go very, very *slowly*. One finger, then two, then three, etc.
- Use lots and lots of water-based lube.
- Cover your partner's hand with a latex glove.
- All fingernails should be short and smooth, even if wearing a glove.
- Remove all jewelry.
- The hand should be inserted and removed very slowly to avoid injury.

Analingus

Commonly known as *rimming,* analingus is the stimulation of the anus with your mouth. Some women and men enjoy the sensation of a wet, warm tongue around the sensitive skin that surrounds the anus.

Hygiene is very important here, so you may want to begin with a bath or shower. The receiver should lie on his or her back with a pillow under the buttocks and knees bent. The giver lies between his or her partner's legs.

Begin with kissing the buttocks and slowly move to the anus. Plant kisses, dry and wet, on the opening to the anus and surrounding skin. Then use your tongue to lick and flick, moving it up and down, side to side, and in circles around the anus. Give some special attention to the perineum, that sensitive spot that lies between his anus and scrotum. If you like, you can even insert your pointed tongue a short distance into the anus.

Here's where it can be fun to play with temperature. Take a small piece of ice in your mouth before licking his anus, then sip some hot tea and return for more. But skip the Altoids; during fellatio that may feel good on his penis, but during analingus it's likely to be a pain in his rear.

Protect Yourself

To avoid getting hepatitis, parasites, and sexually transmitted infections, use a dental dam, a condom that has been cut open, or a piece of plastic wrap over the anus during analingus.

Also remember that the tissue of the rectum is delicate and easily damaged. Forcing any object into your anus and rectum can cause serious, even life-threatening, injury.

IV
. . . . .
Kicking It Up
a Notch

13
. . . . .

Pleasure Enhancers

Now that we've reviewed the basics and explored a few variations on those essential themes, let's go deeper into the pleasure zone. I call the following items—body parts, moves, and accessories—"pleasure enhancers" because they do just that: they help bring us to that deeper level of satisfaction. Some will be familiar, whereas others will seem new and perhaps a bit adventurous. This isn't a list of must-do's but rather an invitation to play, explore, and enjoy. Perhaps, along your path to pleasure, you'll invent a few new pleasure enhancers of your own!

Pleasure Enhancer #1: Kissing

When was the last time you and your partner really kissed? I'm not talking about the perfunctory "Have a nice day, honey" peck but a passionate, romantic, soul-stirring smooch, the kind you two couldn't get enough of when you first met. There is no more intimate an activity than kissing. Unfortunately, for most couples, it is the first intimate act to be lost in a long-term relationship. If your sex life is lacking in fire lately, reinstating kissing is the easiest way to turn up the heat. To help you get started, let's review some kissing basics.

Preparation for Kissing

Lip Care

The lips contain many nerve endings and are covered by a thin layer of skin. The softer and moister you keep your lips, the more responsive they are to stimulation. Dry, rough, chapped lips are no fun for your partner to kiss and provide less pleasure for you. To pamper your pucker:

- Wash your lips every day with a clean, moist washcloth to clean and exfoliate.
- Apply a lip balm every day, especially during the winter months, when lips tend to get chapped.
- Since lips burn easily and sun can dry them out, use a lipstick or lip balm with sunscreen when you're out in the sun, including in the winter.
- Avoid licking your lips; they will dry out.
- Always remove lipstick before going to bed for the night.
- Long-lasting lipsticks tend to be drying, so use in moderation.

Oral Hygiene

Another kiss killer is bad breath. Bad breath occurs when your mouth is dry and stale, such as first thing in the morning or after eating certain foods. Alcohol, smoking, and strong coffee may also give your breath an unpleasant odor. To keep your breath kissably fresh, brush at least twice a day, floss daily, see your dentist regularly, drink lots of water, and eat more raw fruits and veggies.

On days when you are planning to meet your lover, avoid foods like malodorous cheeses, garlic, onion, tuna, anchovies, and salami, which leave oils in your mouth that release odors for hours.

Before lip-locking, it is best to check your breath. (Discreetly lick the back of your hand, move it in front of your nose, and take a whiff.) If your breath fails the sniff test, drink some water or suck on a mint or breath freshener to make your kiss more pleasant.

Kissing 101

The first step to becoming a good kisser is keeping your jaw and lips relaxed. Stiff, pursed lips will make your partner feel like he's kissing a chicken.

Next, part your lips slightly and brush them gently against your partner's lips. Focus on the physical sensation as the nerve endings in your lips are stimulated. Do you feel any stirrings in your genitals?

Take his lower lip gently into your mouth as he takes your upper lip into his and suck very gently. Then switch, taking his upper lip and offering him your lower one.

Slowly open your lips a bit more and extend the tip of your tongue and trace your partner's lips from corner to corner. Now begin tongue play with your partner. The initial contact with his tongue can be quite arousing. Slowly touch and explore each other's tongues: side to side, up and down, and in circles. Great kissing is like a dance where partners share the lead; chase each other playfully.

Extend your tongue a little more and explore his mouth. Slide your tongue along his teeth, gums, and the roof of his mouth. Revel in the various textures, the softness of his lips, the slightly rough texture of his tongue, the smoothness of his teeth. Then retreat and allow him to explore yours.

As important as the tongue is in kissing, a little goes a long way. There is nothing worse than kissing someone whose tongue darts in and out of your mouth and down your throat like a snake. Slow, gentle, intermittent tongue action is so much more romantic.

While kissing, your hands should not be idle. Stroke his face, the back of his head, neck, back. Wrap your arms around his waist or fondle and stroke his buttocks. And while you're letting your fingers do the walking, don't forget to let your partner know how much you are enjoying kissing him. Really get into it. It's not unladylike to moan or sigh, and it will get a rise out of him.

Erotic Body Kissing

Why limit your kissing to the mouth? The entire body is one big pleasure zone covered with nerve endings. Any area of the body is capable of responding to licks, sucks, and gentle bites, so pucker up and start exploring.

Start by planting soft, gentle kisses on his cheeks, eyelids, forehead, earlobes, and neck. Slowly (why rush?) work your way down to his chest, nipples, back, and buttocks. Mix things up a bit by working in some suction with your kisses. This technique is particularly effective when applied to his nipples and buttocks. To really drive him wild, plant a kiss someplace where you've never done so before, perhaps his armpit, the crease of his elbow, the back of his knees, or his toes. Get creative; surprise yourself and him.

Licks and Flicks

After covering his body with kisses, lavish his body with licks. Although most men won't appreciate having their entire faces licked, some do enjoy licks behind and around the ear. Suck gently on his earlobe and trace his ear with the tip of your tongue.

Lick your way down his spine, lingering on the sensitive spot in his lower back where the spine meets the buttocks. Flick your tongue rapidly across his skin; treat him like your personal lollipop. Lick his entire chest. Suck his nipples one at a time. Watch for his reaction. Some men love nipple play, while others become uneasy. Pull his nipple into your mouth and, while holding the suction, flick the tip with your pointed tongue.

Nibbles and Bites

To increase his pleasure, add a few nibbles and passion bites. Cover your teeth with your lips and nibble your way around his body. Then, using the slightest contact with your teeth, place tiny passion bites in sensitive spots like his buttocks and inner thighs. But don't break skin. Human bites are dangerous and require medical attention.

Sexual Enhancer #2: Skin

Your skin is your largest erogenous zone. Its millions of nerve endings are what send those shivers down your spine when your partner kisses your neck and what make you shudder with pleasure when he gently runs his fingertips along your back. Rough, dry skin does not transmit sensations as well as soft skin. Keeping your skin smooth and soft will enhance your pleasure in ways you may not have realized.

Sexy skin care involves taking care of your body inside and out. To nourish your skin from the inside:

- Drink plenty of water to keep skin moist.
- Avoid smoking; it dehydrates the skin.
- Eat a well-balanced diet.

ᑍ Take a multivitamin. You can even find some marketed especially for skin health.

ᑍ Exercise to increase blood flow to the skin and give yourself a rosy glow.

ᑍ Get plenty of sleep.

To take care of your skin from the outside:

ᑍ Use sunscreen every day. Wear it under your makeup, and make putting it on a part of your morning routine.

ᑍ Keep skin clean; washing removes dead skin cells and makes you look and smell fresh.

ᑍ Avoid prolonged hot baths and showers; they can dry your skin out.

ᑍ Use a moisturizing cleansing bar or liquid body wash rather than a harsh soap, and pat—don't rub—skin dry.

ᑍ After your bath or shower, apply a creamy moisturizer to your skin while it is still moist. Unless you have sensitive skin, you might try a deliciously scented lotion or one that has subtly sparkling particles that give skin a glow.

ᑍ Exfoliate regularly using a loofah, buffing pad, or exfoliating cloth to remove dead cells and expose a fresh, new layer of skin. You can also use an exfoliating cream or rub once a week to keep skin smooth. Use a store-bought scrub or make your own. (See my favorite recipe below.)

Pleasure Enhancer #3: The Quickie

There is nothing more delicious than basking in a session of slow leisurely sex. But occasionally you just don't have time or energy for

Hilda's Sexy Exfoliator

1 cup sea salt
½ cup almond oil
¼ cup dark brown sugar
1 tablespoon lemon juice

Mix all the ingredients until thoroughly combined and put them in a pretty jar. To use, gently rub the mixture all over your body, concentrating on rough areas. (Better yet, have your partner do it.) Rinse with warm water; pat dry. Smooth on your favorite moisturizer or oil.

marathon sex, and yes, sometimes even women may not be in the mood for prolonged lovemaking. A quickie may be just what you need. These brief sexual encounters can add spice to your sex life and provide sexual pleasure for you and your partner.

Quickies can be exciting. Consider this: You and your guy are at a party. Your eyes meet, and sparks begin to fly. You must have each other now! You slip away to the bathroom or outside behind the house, unzip his fly, raise your skirt, and move your thong to the side. The sexual urgency and the possibility of getting caught are thrilling. Within minutes it is over, and you both are satisfied—with nothing to give you away except the naughty grins on your faces.

Women need more time to fully enjoy sex, and for that reason quickies should be reserved for the occasional treat. Still, the animalistic quality of a hard-and-fast quickie can be a major turn-on.*

*NOTE: Quickies may not provide enough time for you to lubricate before intercourse. Be sure to use a water-based lubricant to make sex pleasurable.

Pleasure Enhancer #4: Initiating Sex

One of the desires of many men is to have the woman they love initiate sex more often. When you initiate sex, you are saying "I want you. I enjoy sex with you." Everyone wants to feel desired. Think how powerful, sexy, and loved you feel when the man in your life lets you know that he wants you—now. Who wouldn't want that same feeling? Make an effort to tell your man how much he turns you on and find out how such a small gesture can make a big impact on your sex life and your relationship.

Often, women are hesitant to initiate sex because we have been told that only "bad girls" ask for sex. Get over it! You deserve sexual pleasure. We also fear being rejected by our partners. Men risk rejection every time they approach us for sex. It's only fair that we make ourselves vulnerable once in a while as well. So be brave. Go for it!

Not sure how to get started? Well, you can always grab him and kiss him passionately. Grab his crotch or buttocks, and, unless he is clueless, he'll get the idea. Whisper your desire in his ear: "I want you, now!" Climb into bed, naked. Slowly undress in front of him.

The direct approach too difficult for you? Well, you can come up with your own subtle way of letting him know of your desires. Leave a few buttons open on your blouse, wear that perfume that drives him wild, give him a wink and a smile during dinner. But a word of caution: Men are more direct and may not pick up on your more subtle clues. Be sure to let him know that the bowl of strawberries and whipped cream on the bedside table doesn't mean that you are planning to have a snack while reading in bed.

Here are a few seductive tips to get you started:

- While at dinner, slowly and seductively slide your hand up and down your wineglass while gazing into his eyes. The key is to make it look as though you are not aware of what you are doing. The message that he receives will be almost subliminal.

- Kiss the back of his hand, then slip one of his fingers slowly into your mouth. While maintaining suction, slide the finger in and out of your mouth. Explore his finger with your tongue. Eye contact is essential.

- Give him a lap dance. Seat him in a chair while fully clothed. Wear something that makes you feel sexy: a teddy, lacy bra and thong, garter and thigh-high stockings. The rules are that he can watch but not touch. Tease him by dancing seductively in front of him. Straddle him and swivel, shimmy, and swirl your hips on his lap.

- Handcuff and blindfold him. With your pleasure in mind, have your way with him. Be selfish and go for your own pleasure. Let him know how good it feels. Your pleasure will heighten his.

- Meet him at the door and undress him slowly. While edging toward the bedroom, remove one piece of clothing at a time. Drop each piece on the floor as you go, leaving a trail of clothing from the front door to your bed.

- Sometime, make it all about him. Meet him at the door. As soon as he enters, drop to your knees, unzip his pants, remove his penis, and give him a blow job.

- Strip for him. Prepare by choosing slow, erotic music that will be easy to dance to. Purchase undies that make you feel sexy. Red or black G-string and matching bra are a good start. Add a bustier, corset, elbow-length gloves, thigh-high stockings, or garter with stockings for additional drama. It doesn't really matter what you wear on top, since his attention will quickly shift to curiosity about what is underneath. You don't need to be a professional dancer to thrill your man. The key is to move slowly and seductively in front of him. Tease him. Remove your clothes one piece at a time and place them on top of him. When you get down to the last layer, spend some time dancing for him. Make sure he gets a good view of every part of your beautiful body. Slowly remove one of the remaining pieces at a time. Remove your bra or bustier, your stockings, garter, and then the G-string. Enjoy! (You can increase the fantasy by giving him a fistful of dollars before the show, to be placed in your garter as you dance.)

Women who have attended my sex seminars say that this tip did wonders for their self-esteem. The look on their man's face, and the hot sex that followed, made them feel attractive, sexy, seductive, and powerful.

∞ Give him a bath. Place scented candles around the bathroom. Fill the bathtub with warm water. Add bath salts or oils. Sprinkle rose petals on the top. Romantic music will add to the ambience. Escort him to the bathroom and undress him. Place him in the tub and begin to wash his body with a sponge, loofah, or washcloth. Pay particular attention to his back, an area frequently ignored. Be sure to soap and stroke every inch of his body before ending. As he exits the bathtub, wrap him up in a soft, thick bath towel and dry him off.

∞ Give him a pedicure. Fill a plastic tub wide enough to hold both of his feet with warm water. Add scented bath oils or salts. Now place his feet in the tub and allow them to soak. While his feet are soaking, massage his shoulders, neck, and scalp. After ten to fifteen minutes remove one foot from the water. Use both hands to stroke and massage his entire foot. Use a pedicure stone to remove dead skin from the sides and soles of his feet. Then rub the skin with an exfoliating scrub. If needed, clip his toenails. Rinse his feet. Wrap in a warm towel and dry. Using a light oil, continue the foot massage. Place one finger on either side of each toe and pull gently. Hold the ball of the foot with one hand,

and use the other to rotate the ankle slowly. End by lightly kissing each foot.

⊗ Read an erotic story to him in bed before he falls off to sleep. Be expressive, using your voice and body language. Chances are good that he will suddenly find it hard to drift off.

⊗ While at a restaurant, slip your hand under the table and give him a dry hand job. Choose a booth in a private area of the restaurant that makes it less likely that you will be noticed. A tablecloth is a must. Keep zipper closed or you may have problems replacing everything without getting caught. And have a dry napkin available in case of any *spills*.

⊗ While at a formal affair, whisper that you forgot your panties.

⊗ Before going out, slip on a strap-on remote vibrator underneath your panties. When you reach your destination, give him the remote control and a smile. His eyes will not leave you the entire night.

⊗ Flash or moon him when he least expects it.

⊗ Take him shopping for sexy underwear for you.

⊗ Buy him a thong and ask him to model it for you.

⊗ With your digital camera, take a sexy photo of yourself or of a certain body part. Print at home, frame, and place in his briefcase, coat pocket, lunch box, to be found later.

⊗ Send him an erotic e-mail or text message describing what you would like to do to him.*

⊗ Leave a sexy message on his voice mail.

⊗ Read an erotic story together and act out the parts of the main characters.

*NOTE: Use caution if he works for a company that monitors e-mail for security purposes. You want to keep your secret just that, *secret*.

Pleasure Enhancer #5: Pleasure Mapping

Want to increase your partner's pleasure? This exercise, first de-scribed by Dr. Kenneth Ray Stubbs, author of *Erotic Passions,* will help you discover all of your partner's erogenous zones and the types of stimulation that turn him on. First, create a private, warm, quiet environment and have your partner lie down naked on his back. Blindfold him to increase the intensity of his sensations. As you stimulate his body, he should let you know whether he is enjoy-ing the location and type of stimulation that you are providing. Have him rate the sensation from 0 (It doesn't do anything for me) to 3 (I love it!), or simply moan when you've hit the spot.

Explore every inch of his body. Use your fingers, hands, nails, mouth, breath, tongue, and teeth to create pleasure. Experiment with a variety of touching:

- Feathery, light touch with fingertips
- Stroking with hands
- Raking with nails
- Kneading
- Pinching
- Tapping
- Licking
- Biting
- Kissing

Catalog the areas and kind of touch that bring him the most pleasure for future use. When you've covered his whole body, then it's your turn. Exchange places to increase your own pleasure. At the end, you will both know the best "destinations" to bring mutual satisfaction.

Pleasure Enhancer #6: Sexy Oils

Even when your sex life is great, you can find ways to make it even better. I often recommend the following lubricants to add just a touch of spice to your lovemaking.

Zestra is a plant-based oil that increases arousal, vaginal lubrication, and sexual pleasure in some women. The oil is massaged into the clitoris, labia, and opening of the vagina prior to sex. The effects begin five minutes after application and last up to forty-five minutes.

ProSensual is a soy-based lubricant that is described as a topical sexual stimulant for women. When applied to the vulva, it may increase arousal and sexual pleasure. Many women describe a warm tingling sensation after applying ProSensual.

Pleasure Enhancer #7: Erotic Shaving

Shaving your pubic hair may make you feel sexier and just a little bit naughty. The naked skin is also more sensitive to touch, increasing your pleasure. Shave your pubic hair yourself, or you can share the experience with your partner by having him do it for you (if you trust him to stay focused), or you can just let him watch.

Begin by trimming your pubic hair short with sharp scissors, preferably barber shears. Take a warm bath or shower to soften your pubic hair and make it easier to cut. After drying off, lather up with a hypoallergenic shaving cream or gel. There are a variety of shaving products that are made specifically for bikini shaving. Using a new, sharp razor, begin shaving your pubic hair from the bottom and proceed up. Use a light touch and long smooth strokes. It is always best to shave with the grain, but it may be difficult to do so when shaving the bottom of your vulva. Rinse the razor after each stroke to remove hair. Do not go over the same area with the razor more than once or twice. Take your time. Rush, and you may cause injury. Razor nicks in this area are quite uncomfortable.

You can either remove all of the hair or leave a thin strip on the mons. When you're done, rinse your vulva with warm water and pat it dry. Use a blow dryer on cool setting to completely dry the newly shaved skin. Then apply a hypoallergenic moisturizer or lotion.

You can decrease the chance that you will develop annoying razor bumps and ingrown hairs by exfoliating your skin daily with a wet washcloth. Apply a thin layer of 1% hydrocortisone cream (buy at your local pharmacy) immediately after shaving to decrease inflammation that may lead to ingrown hairs. You can also use exfoliating pads daily. (My favorite is Bliss Ingrown Hair Eliminating Peeling Pads.) Wait twenty-four hours after shaving before using.

Bikini Waxing

A longer-lasting alternative is the bikini wax. The Brazilian bikini wax is done at a salon and removes all of the hair on your vulva and around your anus. Warm wax is applied to the hair and covered with small strips of cloth. The cloth is then quickly removed, pulling the hair up from the roots. Expect some discomfort with this procedure. The advantage is that the bikini wax lasts up to five weeks.

An Erotic Shave for Your Man

It shows a tremendous amount of trust if your guy allows you to shave near his most precious possessions. Some men love shaving because it makes the penis look larger.

Begin with a warm shower, or wrap a warm, moist washcloth around his pubic area. Once the hair is soft, trim it with scissors. Lather the hair with shaving cream. Use a sharp razor to remove the hair around his penis. Take your time and use long, slow strokes. As you shave, be sure to tell him how beautiful his penis and scrotum are. I suggest that you skip shaving his scrotum. A nick or cut there can be a disaster!

At the end, use a warm, moist washcloth to remove any stray hair. Then show him how much you like the results.

Pleasure Enhancer #8: Heat

For really hot sex, nothing works like turning up the heat—literally. Heat increases blood flow to your genitals. When your blood flow is increased, your vagina lubricates better, and your tissues become more sensitive. This can lead to better orgasms and increased pleasure.

Prior to sex, sit in a very warm bath or, if available, soak in a Jacuzzi. The increased stimulation from the jets will enhance the effects of the warm water. No time for a bath? Take a warm, moist washcloth and place it over your vulva for a few minutes. Or if you have a hot-water bottle, discover why it is useful for more than just menstrual cramps: Fill it with warm water and sit on it or lie down and rest it on your vulva and clitoris.

Want to share the heat with him? Wrap a clean, thick, warm, moist hand towel around his penis before a hand or blow job.

Pleasure Enhancer #9: Role Playing

Act out your fantasy. You won't believe how arousing and sexually stimulating it can be. Sex should be fun, and what better way to have fun than to step outside the box and engage in role playing? Here are some suggestions to get you going:

One-night stand. Dress in something sexy, go to a bar, and wait for your man. Have him pretend to be a stranger and pick you up.

Lady of the night. Dress provocatively and stand and wait at a corner. Then your husband drives by and picks you up. Check into a motel for urgent sex. Watch out for cops!

Doctor and patient. One of you is the patient and dresses only in a robe. The other acts as the doctor and must give the patient a very thorough examination.

Workout routine. He dresses like a personal trainer in shorts (spandex preferred) and tight tank top or T-shirt. You play a lonely amorous housewife. He takes you through a very tough, sweaty workout routine. Flexibility a must.

Sex-o-gram. Dress in a costume of your choice. You arrive at the front door and ring the doorbell. When your mate answers, enter and begin an erotic dance and striptease. What a great way to say "Happy Birthday," or just "Hello."

Teacher and student. Ever have a crush on a teacher? Now is the time to relive that fantasy. One of you acts as teacher, the other, as adoring and willing pupil.

Pleasure Enhancer #10: Lubricants

Lubricants are underappreciated treats. Not only are they useful in replacing moisture when your vagina is dry, but they also can increase the sensitivity of your genitals and, thereby, your pleasure. And for those all-night sex sessions, lubricants can help decrease postsex soreness and friction caused by drying.

Lubricants are a must anytime that you engage in anal sex or toy play. When used for intercourse, lubricants should be applied during foreplay. Ask your partner to rub the lubricant on your vulva and slide some inside your vagina. Then slather a generous amount along the entire length of his penis.

Here are a few of my favorites:

Astroglide is one of the most popular water-based lubricants. It contains glycerin, a sugar, and has a slightly sweet taste. It also comes in a strawberry flavor. You can find it in your local pharmacy, and it is reasonably priced.

Eros is a clear, long-lasting lube that is silicone based and has an oily texture. It has no taste, but the oily texture makes it unpleasant to use before oral sex. It is great for sex play in the water and anal sex.

Liquid Silk is a creamy, smooth, odorless lube that does not contain glycerin and has a slightly bitter taste.

Sylk is considered a "natural" lube. It contains only a kiwi extract, water, and a small amount of preservative. It is wonderful for women with sensitive skin. It has a slightly bitter taste.

Wet Platinum is a silicone-based, long-lasting lube that is great for sex in the shower or Jacuzzi and anal sex. The taste, however, is terrible.

KY Liquid is a thin, clear, odorless lube that contains glycerin and has a slightly sweet flavor. You can find it in your local pharmacy.

KY Warming Liquid is a clear, odorless liquid with a slightly sweet taste. When placed on your genitals, it feels warm and wet. The warmth is quite arousing and, for some women, will increase their natural vaginal secretions. It is available at your local pharmacy.

Vagisil Intimate Lubricant is a light, odorless, tasteless lube that contains vitamin E and aloe. You can find it in your local pharmacy.*

*NOTE: If you are prone to vaginal yeast infections, you should avoid lubes that contain glycerin, a form of sugar. Silicone-based lubes should not be used with toys made of silicone because they will bond with them and cause discomfort when you manipulate the toy.

Pleasure Enhancer #11: Sharing the Sisterhood

Have you ever shared sexual secrets with your best girlfriend? Most of us have not. Perhaps we fear what our friends will think of us. In my opinion, this is an untapped resource for many women in their quest for sexual knowledge and pleasure. What better way to increase your sexual knowledge and confidence than by talking to other women? Women are natural healers and educators. Each of us carries a tremendous amount of knowledge that, when shared with others, can be life altering. One way to tap into this powerful and underused resource is to form sisterhood groups to share and discuss sexual experiences, thoughts, tips, and fantasies. Through this bonding, women become sounding boards and valuable resources for each other. Many women find that forming sister circles can help break down their inhibitions, making it easier to get in touch with their sexual feelings.

To form your sisterhood group, you will need to invite a group of women whom you like and trust. It will be important to create a supportive, trusting environment in which each woman feels free to explore her sexual feelings and thoughts and in which all discussions are nonjudgmental and supportive. To ensure that your circle meets regularly, schedule monthly or bimonthly meetings and serve plenty of food and drinks to create a festive and fun atmosphere. Once you have formed your group, here are some suggestions for sharing:

Fantasy Parties

Each sisterhood member is responsible for writing her own erotic fantasy. When she arrives at the party, the fantasy is placed in a large bowl, so it is anonymous. After girl talk, fellowship, food, and a few glasses of wine, it is time to read the fantasies. Each member will take turns reading a fantasy aloud to the group. Be ready for laughs and enlightenment. You will be surprised at how much you can learn about sex by listening to someone else's fantasy. By the end of the party, each woman won't be able to wait to get home to her partner.

Pleasure Parties

Invite a local adult-store or Passion Party representative (see "Resources") to give a presentation on erotic toys to your group. The sales associate will display erotic toys, explain how they work, and offer them for sale to the group. This can be a great learning experience for all.

Field Trip

You and a group of girlfriends take a trip to a local, or not so local, adult store to explore, sample, and purchase. Take advantage of the immense knowledge of the sales associates in the store.

"Recipe" Swap

Invite the group over for tea and have each woman anonymously (or not so anonymously) write her favorite sexual technique on a recipe card. Place the cards in a bowl. When you are all ready, take turns reading the cards out loud. The hostess is responsible for typing all of the tips and sending them to each member for future reference.

Book of the Month

The group can choose a sexy book—erotica, sex manual, romantic novel—for the group to read and discuss. Alternatively, each member can take turns reading a sexy book and presenting interesting new information derived from the book to the group.

Sexual Enhancer #12: Making Your Own Erotic Movie

Boost your arousal and pleasure by making your own erotic movie. Place a video camera on a tripod, point the lens toward the bed, and videotape your lovemaking session. Keep your one and only copy under lock and key until ready for viewing. (You wouldn't want it to end up on the Internet!) Too shy for the big screen? Place a tape recorder at the head of your bed and record your sexy sounds during lovemaking. Listen together later to put you in a sexy mood.

Sexual Enhancer #13: Aromatherapy

For centuries, scents have been used to increase sexual desire and pleasure. Here's why: Scents enter your nose and are carried to your brain's emotional center, where they can stimulate memories, emotions, and moods. They can soothe, relax, energize, and arouse.

Fragrant essential oils can increase your arousal and pleasure as well as that of your partner. Use a diffuser to scent a room, add oils to your bath, or sprinkle a few drops on your bed linens and pillows.

Use any of the following essential oils to add spice to your sex life. Each can be used alone or make your own sexy blend.

Ylang-ylang soothes, calms, and decreases anxiety. It has a sweet scent that has been described as "seductive," and is thought to increase sexual desire.

Sandalwood has been used as an aphrodisiac since ancient times. Its musklike scent creates a sense of euphoria in men and women. It is said to increase arousal in men and pleasure in women.

Rose, considered the fragrance of love, is thought to be a sexual stimulant for women. The sweet scent of the rose decreases anxiety and promotes feelings of well-being.

Lavender relaxes and calms. It has also been shown to increase arousal in men.

Jasmine has been used to increase sexual desire and pleasure since ancient times. The sweet scent relaxes and soothes, making it easier for couples to get in the mood for lovemaking. The scent is seductive and makes couples feel closer to each other. It may also help treat male sexual problems like impotence and low desire.

Pleasure Enhancer #14: Burning Your Panties

In my opinion, panties should be banned. Going pantiless decreases your risk of vaginal infections, keeps you in touch with your body, and makes you feel more comfortable with one of your most important parts, your genitals. If you're unsure or skittish about going "commando," try it at home first. Delight in the sensual feeling of the air flowing over you as you move and of the various textures against your skin. Once you give going pantiless a try, you may never go back. Besides, it makes quickies that much quicker. So burn your panties and free your genitals from bondage!

Pleasure Enhancer #15: Noisy Sex

Many of us are accustomed to remaining silent during sex because of our early experiences. Perhaps it was the fear of being caught by parents, roommates, or friends while masturbating or making out that silenced you back then. Old habits are hard to break, but learning to be more expressive in bed will greatly enhance your pleasure. Release your inhibitions slowly. Begin by practicing the breath. Allow yourself to make noise as you exhale (*ah-h-h-h*). As you become more relaxed, you can add sighs, pants, groans, moans, and screams. When you really feel free to be expressive, add words and phrases that describe the pleasure you are receiving. Making noise will increase the intensity of your orgasms. It will enhance not only your pleasure but also that of your partner. So go ahead, speak up.

Pleasure Enhancer #16: Picasso Anyone?

Finger painting was never more fun than when you create a masterpiece using your partner as a canvas. Use edible body paint (available at adult stores) or go all natural and use a variety of sauces—chocolate, strawberry, and caramel come to mind. Be creative and spread your work of art over a wide area of his body. When removing, start north and lick your way south.*

*CAUTION: Do not put anything in the vagina that will be difficult to remove completely. Sweet sauces in the vagina can cause an infection.

Pleasure Enhancer #17: Erotic Phone Talk

When you and your honey are separated, keep the fires burning by indulging in a little aural sex with your partner. Phone sex can enhance intimacy and increase arousal. The resulting anticipation of future intimate acts with your partner can elevate your sex life to new levels of pleasure.

In order to give, and get, good phone sex, start by setting the mood as if you and your partner were physically together. Dim the lights or light scented candles. Pop your favorite slow jam or soft music into the CD player. Close your eyes and visualize your partner. If you like, you can remove your clothes before the call, or wait until your partner gives you instructions to remove them one piece at a time.

Phone sex is a fantasy, so feel free to use your imagination. You can describe in detail the last time the two of you were intimate. In your most sultry voice, share your fantasy about what you plan to do the next time you see each other. For a really memorable experience, give each other sexual instructions and act them out. Tell your partner what, when, where, and how to touch his various body parts. Ask him to tell you what he is doing and what it feels like. Then it's your turn. This is not the time for silent orgasms. The sound of your ecstasy will bring such pleasure to your partner.

Be aware that if you are using an analog cordless phone, your hot conversation may be overheard by a nearby baby monitor or radio scanner. So unless you want to risk getting some strange looks from your neighbors, you may want to invest in a digital cordless or use a noncordless phone.

Pleasure Enhancer #18: Slip and Slide

Take turns massaging and spreading massage oil over each other's bodies. Once covered, slide your bodies all over each other. Front to front, front to back, and—for laughs—back to back. The feeling of slick skin sliding across slick skin can be indescribably sensuous. Experiment with different types of oils: scented, flavored, self-heating. Finish in the shower.

Pleasure Enhancer #19: New Techniques

Purchase a new sex manual and two highlighters, one pink and one blue. Take turns reading the manual, highlighting all of the activities that you would like to try. Each week, one of you is responsible for perfecting one of the techniques chosen by the other.

Pleasure Enhancer #20: Urgent Sex

Remember that hot scene in your favorite movie where the couple was so horny they practically ripped each other's clothes off? Or maybe you've had a sexual experience when the urge to merge was so intense that you didn't take the time to remove your clothes? Re-create that electricity by having sex with your clothes on. Meet him at the door, reach down into his pants, and grab his penis. Unzip his pants, drop your panties, and make love against the wall. Or straddle him while he is sitting in a sturdy chair or couch. You can try this move in front of a full-length mirror either facing him or facing away from him. To take it to another level, fantasize that you could be discovered.

Pleasure Enhancer #21: Pleasure Pack

Create a pleasure pack and keep it next to your bed. Fill it with lubricated latex and flavored condoms, a variety of water-based lubricants—flavored, warming, clear, and colored—small toys for him and her, and a scented candle. (If you have children, place your treasure trove in a small locked box out of reach.)

Pleasure Enhancer #22: Change of Venue

Having sex in the same bed night after night can become boring. To fight boredom and rekindle the flames of desire, have sex in new and exciting places. A change as simple as having sex in a different room—the kitchen, bathroom, walk-in closet, foyer, or balcony—can be very exciting. Sex in the backseat of your car can bring back the excitement of your youth. And if you are afraid of getting caught, park your car in your driveway or garage and fantasize that you are in lovers' lane. Pitch a tent or share a sleeping bag in your backyard and make love in the grass.

Pleasure Enhancer #23: Talking Dirty

If you're anything like me, just thinking about talking dirty can make you cringe with embarrassment. But what I learned—and so can you—is that once you let down your guard and give it a try, indulging in this very private erotic banter can be quite arousing.

A change in attitude might be useful in getting over being self-conscious about erotic talk. Even though we call it talking dirty, it's not something that should cause shame. When done within the confines of a healthy sexual relationship, with a partner whom you trust and with the understanding that what is said is to remain just between the two of you, it can actually be liberating.

There are other benefits to adding erotic dialogue to your bedroom routine. Consider:

- Dirty talk enhances communication with your partner. It is a sexy way to express your needs and desires and may also provide the spark that you need to increase the passion in your relationship and improve your sex life.
- Using sexy words can serve as a powerful aphrodisiac, conjuring up all sorts of delicious fantasies.
- It can decrease your inhibitions, making it easier for you to let go, thereby increasing your pleasure
- Dirty talk can make you feel sexier and more confident. What man can resist a woman who is secure enough to ask for what she wants in a sexy and erotic way? And tapping into that sexual power can be a major turn-on.

Say What?

Now that you've decided to incorporate dirty talk into your sex play, the next step is figuring out what to say and when to say it. Keep in mind there are no rules. This is sex play; it's supposed to be fun.

You can get the game started by firing up your imagination, and your partner's arousal, long before you get to the bedroom. Send him an e-mail or text message, leave him a suggestive voice mail, or write a sexy note and leave it in his coat pocket to be discovered later. You may find it easier to write dirty than talk dirty in the beginning.

If your partner has used erotic phrases in the past, you can feel comfortable reciprocating. But if the only words he uses to describe sexual anatomy are *penis* and *vagina,* you may need to start slowly and feel him out before advancing to more graphic language.

To help find the right phrases, begin by reading erotic stories out loud, with and without your partner. Rent an erotic movie. Take note of those sexy phrases that turn you on. Be very selective in the phrases that you choose to copy, as the point is not to sound like a porn star but a confident, sensual woman who feels comfortable with her sexual side. Call a phone sex chat line and take notes. It can be expensive, but done once it could also be a good learning experience.

If you're feeling at all hesitant about beginning to talk dirty, practice saying sexy words aloud to yourself until they flow off your tongue, before using with a partner. Most important, give yourself permission to step outside your comfort zone. Be daring, adventurous, provocative, seductive, sexy.

Pleasure Enhancer #24: Re-creating Your First Time

For most couples, the most magical, memorable, and exciting shared sexual experience was the first time they had sex. The chemicals and hormones that are at their peak in the beginning of a relationship, and the thrill of a new experience, all increase the intensity of any physical or emotional sensations that are produced. With that in mind, think back and write an erotic story describing the first time that the two of you made love. Recall every single detail: how you looked, felt, tasted, sounded, smelled. Go back to that moment in your mind and put it all on paper. This exercise will jump-start your libido and elevate your lovemaking to new heights.

One couple told me that they had the best sex they'd had in five years after completing this exercise. Taking it one step further, they returned to the location of their first mating. Reliving the first time brought back memories of how hot their sex life had been in the beginning of their marriage. It provided the incentive that they needed to spend more time on their love life and increase their emotional bond.

14
. . . . .

The Big O

Orgasms are throbbing, pulsating pleasure. For a few seconds, you let go, lose all control, and enter a different state of consciousness. It is fleeting and wonderful. Yet, in my experience, nothing causes women more angst. As has always been the case for men, achieving orgasm has become a sexual goal for many women. And not just any orgasm; it must be the *right* orgasm. It must be mind-blowing, prolonged, and multiple and must occur during intercourse—and every time. When sexual encounters don't end with the perfect orgasmic experience, women—and their partners—may feel like failures.

Orgasms are wonderful, but sometimes we focus so much on the goal of orgasm, that we lose much of the pleasure of sexual intimacy. In many ways, the journey toward orgasm is so much better than the actual event. It is on the journey that you share the merging of bodies, minds, and breath.

Sex is about pleasure: giving it, receiving it, sharing it. When you take away the pressure to achieve the perfect orgasm, or any orgasm at all, you allow your body and mind to bask in the pleasure that the two of you are creating. Many women are perfectly satisfied without orgasm, and some women who experience orgasm are not truly satisfied.

An Orgasm Is . . .

Physically, an orgasm is a series of rhythmic contractions of the uterus, lower vagina, and pelvic floor muscles, which lead to a release of sexual tension. Some women have orgasms that are centered in the pelvis, while others may experience mental imagery or auras. Every woman's experience of orgasm is different, and that experience may vary from one encounter to the next for the same woman. Each woman is unique. Honor your own sexual experience and pleasure by not comparing your experience to some mythic standard of perfection. Instead, discover what gives *you* pleasure.

The Key to Orgasm Is . . .

There are those who say that the key to achieving orgasm is stimulation of the clitoris. Yet some women don't experience much pleasure from clitoral stimulation. Some say that the vagina is the most important element. Yet there are women who are able to achieve orgasm without touching the vagina at all. Stimulating the nipples, cervix, or lips can bring some people to climax. Dr. Beverly Whipple, through her research, has shown that some women can even achieve orgasm through fantasy alone. The point is, *there is no one way to experience orgasm.* The way *you* experience that level of sexual pleasure is as individual as you are. So experiment, keep an open mind, and enjoy your research.

How to Get It . . .

You cannot will an orgasm any more than you can will yourself to be younger or taller. But you *can* set up conditions that will make experiencing a level of pleasure that may climax in orgasm more likely.

Many women have told me that they experienced their first orgasm after reading *What Your Mother Never Told You About S-e-x*. For some, it was being educated about their body parts and how those parts work; for others, it was being given permission to explore their bodies and to self-pleasure; and for still others it was rejecting the pressure to perform for themselves or their partners that was the tipping point that led to orgasmic bliss.

Female orgasms are complicated and have emotional, mental, and physical components. In my opinion, they are also a learned response, meaning that you need to learn what feels good and how to let go. You may also need to *un*-learn negative sexual messages you may have received during childhood that interfere with your pleasure.

Here are a few things that you can do to increase your orgasm potential. Remember, easy does it.

⬧ Ironically, perhaps the most important thing you can do is to let go and stop trying so hard. That's right. The key to orgasm is *not* to try to have one. When you pressure yourself, and focus on the goal of orgasm, you risk increasing your anxiety and short-circuiting your pleasure and orgasmic response. Instead of pleasure, you are consumed with fear (that you will not achieve your goal) and anxiety (that you will disappoint your partner). A recent study that scanned women's brains during orgasm confirmed the obvious: to enjoy sex and experience orgasm, women must be relaxed and free of anxiety, fear, and worry. Sex is not a performance, test, or competition. Decrease the pressure to perform. Relax and focus on the emotional, spiritual, and physical pleasures of lovemaking.

∞ Get to know your body parts and how they respond. That means that you must spend time discovering your pleasure zones through self-pleasuring. Often women do not reach the ultimate heights of sexual pleasure because they are not receiving the right type of stimulation for an adequate amount of time. When you self-pleasure, you are in control. You can stimulate your most sensitive areas in the way that gives you the most pleasure for as long as you desire. To help you on your way, review chapters 2 and 5 of this book.

∞ Add toys to self-pleasuring and sex with your partner. If you have never achieved orgasm, I recommend the Hitachi Magic Wand. The intense vibrations that this toy provides will almost certainly send you over the edge. See chapter 15 for more about toys. A new device, *Vielle,* is a plastic finger cot-shaped device that has multiple nodules on its surface. Worn on the finger, it is used to stimulate your clitoris and the rest of your vulva. It has been shown to increase the number of orgasms and satisfaction.

∞ Nurture an active fantasy life. During sex, allow your brain to create sexy thoughts that increase your arousal and keep you focused on sex and the pleasurable sensations that you are feeling. (See chapter 17 for more on fantasies.)

∞ Practice your Kegel exercises every day. Exercising your pelvic floor muscles makes them stronger and increases the blood flow to your pelvis. Not only may you achieve more orgasms, but they will be more intense. Squeeze your PC muscle during self-stimulation and sexual intercourse to increase your pleasure. (See chapter 6 for information on Kegel exercises.)

Self-Pleasuring

Many women in my sex seminars have told me that the hand-held shower massage is the most effective method of experiencing orgasm during self-pleasuring. The pulsations created by the showerhead can be adjusted and the warmth of the water increases blood flow to your genitals, increasing your arousal. Begin your shower play with your legs closed. Direct a gentle spray on your mons and labia. As you become more aroused, you can part your legs farther and increase the intensity of the water pulsations. Begin to move the showerhead up and down, side to side, or in circles. If you feel comfortable, you can direct the flow against your clitoris. Relax and breathe. Enjoy!

- Be patient. Sex improves as we age and become more comfortable with ourselves and our sexuality. I tell my patients that, although every woman is different, many women don't truly learn to create and accept the highest level of pleasure (and orgasm) until they near the age of thirty.
- Learn to relinquish control and let go. Breathe. Go with the wonderful physical and emotional sensations. Accept pleasure. You deserve it!

A Tip to Intensify Your Orgasm

When self-stimulating, or during sex if you have a disciplined and cooperative partner, bring yourself to the brink of orgasm but stop all stimulation before you come. Wait for a minute, then resume stimulation. Again stop just before you reach orgasm. Bring yourself to the edge of orgasm and back several times before allowing the sexual tension to be released through an intense, all-consuming orgasm.

Dr. Hil says:

Women's experience of sex has been based on the male model: desire, arousal, orgasm. Women's sexual response and satisfaction is much more complicated. It is time that we change the big "O" to the big "P." The very best, *ultimate* sex is about pleasure.

V

. . . . .

Adding Some Extra Spice

15
. . . . .

Tempting
Titillating Toys

I think every woman should own at least one sex toy for private pleasuring or for enhancing sex play with her partner. Sensual playthings can help you gain a better understanding of your own body, explore your sexual preferences, find new ways to achieve ultimate pleasure, and heighten your sexual experience overall. If you don't explore, how will you discover the full depths of your sexuality: what turns you on and brings you satisfaction? Experimenting with toys when you're alone is a way to take control of your sexual experience, which can lead to greater confidence and better sex when you're with a partner. Bringing your sex toys and games along when you're with someone can add a wonderful form of play to the experience.

Using sex toys doesn't mean you're not able to have pleasurable sexual experiences without them. Think of them as an accessory: The same way you'd add a gorgeous piece of jewelry to enhance a great outfit, using toys and games during sex just spices up the whole experience and makes it that much more interesting, pleasurable, and fun.

We'll take a look at the most popular and widely available toys and games you might want to try and give you some sexy ideas for what to do with them. Keep an open mind and see which ones pique your interest. Just the idea of using some of these toys can be a bit of a turn-on. Then again, some of them may be of no interest to you at all. What excites someone else may leave you cold. Experiment, communicate, and find which toys and games are right for you and your partner.

Where the Toys Are

When we talk about *sex toys,* the vibrator is just the tip of the sexual iceberg; the term encompasses all kinds of manual and mechanical devices. In fact, with a little imagination, almost anything can be used to add a little fun to the sexual experience. Since ancient times, people have been using all sorts of simple, sensual tools for sex play: tickling their partner with a feather or using their own hair to stroke him; pouring honey, wine, melted chocolate, or the juice of luscious fruits on his body and then licking it off. Fruits, vegetables, or anything long and cylindrical would allow one person to penetrate another. In fact, anything that can be used to heighten the senses, tease, or please the other person can be classified as a sex toy.

Thanks to the existence of sex shops designed for female shoppers, women have a safe, comfortable shopping environment for such equipment. Woman-centered erotica stores encourage their customers—the majority female—to pick up the toys, feel, and play with them.

Aside from the sex shops, there are plenty of other safe, comfortable places to purchase adult toys. You can throw or attend erotica parties (think sexy Tupperware party), where you can get a close-up of the wide variety of sex enhancers in the privacy of someone's home, and place an order before you leave. And if you want total privacy when you shop, you can order toys over the Internet or through mail-order catalogs.

Myths and Misunderstandings

If false ideas are floating around in the back of your mind, you're not going to be comfortable experimenting with toys, and you're going to miss out on a whole lot of fun. So, before we take a look at toys, let's debunk some myths you may have heard.

- **Myth #1: Sex toys are for women only.** False. Most people think that only women use vibrators. Men also can use vibrators—and they do. Vibrators can also increase pleasure during couples' play.

- **Myth #2: Once you start using them, you won't want to experience sex with a real person.** False. Toys add another dimension to your sex life, but a toy can't replace a loving, passionate interaction with a partner. Most people want both. Fortunately, the more you learn about how to use your toys, the more new techniques you'll have to share with the mate in your life.

- **Myth #3: Using a vibrator will make it impossible to experience an orgasm without it.** Also false. As with anything pleasurable, it's possible to develop an attachment to your vibrator. If you use it often, you will get used to the high-intensity stimulation and rapid orgasms that the vibrator provides, but it doesn't mean that you won't be able to have pleasurable sex without it. If you do notice a change in your ability to have an orgasm without the vibrator, it may help to take a break from the vibrator for a few days before having sex with a partner.

⊗ **Myth #4: After using sex toys, "ordinary" sex is boring.** False. Most people who use sex toys consider them fun additions to their sex lives—a little variety. Toys can actually make "ordinary" sex "extraordinary" by helping you explore your own and your partner's sensual likes and dislikes, learn how to experience orgasms, and get more creative in your sex play. It wakes you up sensually, so that even when you don't have toys to play with, sex is better.

⊗ **Myth #5: Using a sex toy is unnatural.** False. Sexual fulfillment is a natural part of human experience that should be enjoyed by everyone. If toys can help you improve your lovemaking without harming yourself or anyone else, then why shouldn't you benefit from toy play?

⊗ **Myth #6: Vibrators will make your genitals numb.** If you leave a vibrator in one spot for a prolonged period of time, you may experience temporary numbness, but it will resolve itself soon after the vibrator is removed. Vibrators won't permanently change the sensitivity of your sex organs.

If you're open to adding a little something extra to your sexual play by turning to toys, prepare yourself for a world of new and exciting possibilities. But if you find that you just can't get comfortable with using toys, then don't add them to your sexual experience. It's your choice. The thing to remember—and this goes for all things sexual—is that you don't have to—and shouldn't—do anything that's not comfortable and pleasurable for both you and your partner.

Dr. Hil says:

Every woman should own at least one sex toy. Here's why: Sex toys (1) are available whenever you are; (2) never get tired, never have a bad day at the office, or prefer to watch the football game; (3) have staying power and can last as long as you want them to as long as you keep an extra set of batteries around; (4) won't roll over and fall asleep; (5) can give you a multitude of new thrills; (6) are "safe" (as long as you don't share); (7) and you don't have to worry about whether he will call you tomorrow.

What Are Toys Made Of?

When you walk into your neighborhood sex shop, you're going to see sex toys made of everything from plastic to rubber to glass and steel. How will you decide which one to choose? Consider how comfortable it will be to use, how realistic you want it to be, and how easy it will be to care for. Here's a guide to what's what.

- **Jelly rubber** is a porous rubber blend that has a soft feel that many women like. Unfortunately, it can become difficult to clean over time since lubricants and body fluids can get trapped in the pores and get sticky. It tends to hold its vibrations better than rubber latex. Clean with soap and water.

- **Cyberskin** is realistic looking and feeling, but it's very high maintenance. Toys made of this material are very porous, difficult to clean, and get sticky after cleaning. To maintain the soft skinlike feel, it helps if you cover them with cornstarch when you store them. Bacteria and yeast can get trapped in them and may cause chronic vaginal infections. Your best bet is to use condoms with vibrators or dildos made of jelly rubber or cyberskin. Even so, you may find that you need to replace these toys more often than toys made of other materials. Cover with a condom to keep clean.

❧ **Glass** is used most often for dildos, a type that is great for G-spot stimulation. They can be warmed or chilled for different sensations, and the nonporous material is easy to clean. Most will claim to be shatterproof, but be careful because rough handling can cause them to break. Glass toys are often hand blown and quite beautiful. You could probably put one on your coffee table, and no one would know it was a sex toy. Clean with soap and water.

❧ **Plastic** is nonporous, hard, durable, and easy to clean. You can warm it with hot water before you use it for a more realistic feel. Plastic is the best material for really intense vibrations, but makes for louder toys. Clean with soap and water.

❧ **Steel** can also be warmed or heated, and it's also nonporous, so it's easy to clean. However, the feel is far from realistic.

❧ **Silicone** is the most popular material for sex toys, perhaps because it warms up to body temperature, maintains heat, and is easy to clean. If it's waterproof, you can boil it for three minutes to sterilize it or put it in the dishwasher. Toys made of silicone can last a long time. Just be sure not to use them with silicone-based lubricants; silicone-based lubricants damage silicone toys.

Good Vibrations

Vibrators are among the most widely used and widely available toys, and because they come in such a variety of sizes, shapes, colors, and materials, you're sure to find one that you're comfortable with. They're great for vaginal, clitoral, or anal stimulation and also can be used internally, externally, or both. Some vibrators also serve as body massagers, relieving more than just your sexual tension.

There are vibrators that work by battery; others plug into the nearest electrical socket. There's even a model that can be plugged into the cigarette lighter of your car.

Selecting the Right Model

Finding the right vibrator may take a little self-loving homework. As you look at the variety of toys, think about what you like sexually and ask yourself a few questions:

Do I like penetration, clitoral stimulation, or both?

When you're having sex, do you find it most stimulating when your partner plays with your clitoris, penetrates your vagina, or both? Your answer will help you determine which type of vibrator you'll like best. Some vibrators are made for external use only to stimulate your clitoris; others are designed to enter your vagina; and some can stimulate both, sometimes at the same time.

Do I need a lot of power or something less intense?

All vibes are not created equal. Before you buy, consider the intensity of the vibration that will pleasure you. An electric vibrator, for example, produces strong vibration and won't run out of energy as a battery-powered one eventually will. It is typically more expensive than its battery-powered counterpart, but it may be worth the investment if you plan to use it often or for long periods of time.

The best way to find the vibe that's right for you is to find a retailer that has a large selection of toys and that will let you handle and "test" the goods.

Which toy do you find aesthetically pleasing?

Yes, you have to be attracted to your toys. If you don't like the way a vibrator looks, it's going to be very difficult for you to get comfortable using it. Want something that looks and feels like the real thing? Pick a vibrator that looks like an actual penis. A woman who wants to be more discreet can find something as unassuming as a tube of lipstick.

Getting to Know Your Vibrator

Once you've chosen your vibrator, it's time to get to know it a little more intimately. I suggest you experiment with your new toy by yourself initially, so you can figure out what works best for you before you share it with your partner. Find a comfortable, private place and carve out some quiet time so that you can take your time and enjoy your self-pleasuring without being disturbed. To increase your pleasure and prevent friction burns, use some water-based lubricant to generously moisten your vagina and vulva as well as the vibrator itself. For the most pleasure, keep your lubricant at room temperature or a little warmer. If you have a battery-operated vibrator, you can warm the end of it with water.

If you're a beginner, lie on your back with your legs straight and slightly parted. With your vibrator on a low setting, slowly and gently move it across your body, down your labia, and across your mons. If the vibration is too strong or uncomfortable, stop and lower the setting or cover your vulva with a cloth to decrease the intensity.

As you become more aroused, you can open your legs and bend your knees to expose more of your clitoris and vulva. Experiment with the speeds as well as the amount of pressure you use. Do what feels good to you, whether it's putting the vibrator directly on your clitoris or alongside it. If you have a penis-shaped vibrator or smoothie, you may enjoy vaginal penetration. As always, don't feel any pressure to have an orgasm, just concentrate on doing what feels good to you.

The Dildo

Vibrators may generally be the most popular sex toys, but dildos—nonmotorized, penis-shaped toys—are an age-old favorite. Even before electricity was ever discovered, inventive and resourceful women were secretly using all kinds of smooth, cylindrical objects, from stones to squashes, for self-pleasuring. Over time, these playthings evolved into the wide variety of anatomically correct dildos you'll find in sex shops today.

If dildos offer an advantage over vibrators it's that, because they're manual, you have complete control of your sexual experience: You control the motion and speed of the toy. You determine whether to use it for penetration or external clitoral stimulation—or both. Despite the fact that dildos may seem to have fewer "bells and whistles," they can offer you a wide-ranging sexual experience and can be used solo or with a partner. Just use your imagination.

Selecting the Right Model

Given the wide variety of dildos available, how do you choose one that's right for you? It really comes down to aesthetics, size, and the way you plan to use it. Visit your local sex shop and take a look around. See which dildos attract your attention.

If you're going for something that's anatomically realistic, visualize the perfect penis, thinking about it in terms of size, shape, thickness, and texture, and look for something that matches your ideal. Or you may like a dildo that's more sculptural, something you could leave on your nightstand like a piece of art.

Think about how you're going to use the dildo: alone or with a partner. Those considerations will help you decide whether to choose something that looks like a real penis or only vaguely phallic, a hand-held dildo or one that attaches to a harness, a two-headed dildo or one that curves.

Are you a sex-toy novice? If so, you may want to opt for a smaller dildo until you get comfortable with your new toy. Remember, bigger isn't always better, so concentrate on finding a dildo that's right for you.

Doing It with Your Dildo

When you bring your dildo home, get to know it before you take it to bed. Examine it and handle it, getting a sense of its size, weight, and texture. Imagine how you might use it for pleasuring yourself or your partner. Then get a little more intimate with it.

When using a dildo, always apply lots of lubricant to your vulva, vagina, and the toy. Explore your mons and labia with the dildo. Experiment with different speeds and pressures as you stroke your clitoris. If you decide to penetrate your vagina, wait until you're aroused, then enter slowly. Keep the dildo in the lower part of your vagina initially; as you start to feel more sensual, you can slide it deeper into your vagina, moving it around to stimulate your most sensitive areas. You might stimulate your nipples and breasts to heighten arousal. Want to share the experience? You certainly can. Have your partner use the dildo on you in much the same way you'd use it on yourself.

Toys for Boys

When it comes to sex toys, the rules of the playground still apply: share your toys and play nicely with others. What I mean by that is, let your partner in on the fun. Many men find using toys in sex play incredibly stimulating. You can use your vibrator or dildo to

The Ten Toys That Every Woman Should Own

1. **The Pocket Rocket.** If you can buy only one toy, this is the one. It is small enough to fit in your purse and quite discreet. In fact, it looks more like a tube of lipstick than a sex toy. Despite its petite size, it is quite powerful. The pocket rocket is great for travel and so common that airport security screeners no longer ask questions when they discover one in your carry-on bags. Lubricate well and use to stimulate your labia and clitoris.

2. **The Hitachi Magic Wand.** This is a large electric vibrator that is just as effective relaxing tired, sore back muscles as producing intense orgasms. It is sold in the small-appliance section of many department stores as well as in adult sex shops. The vibrations of the soft, rounded head are so intense that you may need to cover your vulva with a small towel before touching them with the vibrator. The long handle makes it perfect for couples sex play. For instance, place it between you and your lover while in the sitting position. This vibrator is perfect for the woman who has

continued

never experienced an orgasm or is menopausal and needs more intense stimulation.

3. **A dual-action vibrator.** Sold under several brand names, including the Rabbit, made famous by the *Sex and the City* television show, the dual vibrator is the ultimate in sex toys. I would not recommend it for beginners, or for those who are squeamish about trying sex toys. It is the only toy that stimulates multiple areas of your vulva and vagina at the same time (all while running on four AA batteries!). The shaft twirls inside your vagina and stimulates your G-spot as well as the sensitive areas surrounding your cervix. The pearls near the base of the shaft tumble to stimulate the sensitive entrance and lower third of your vagina. And the critter attached to the shaft flutters and vibrates against your clitoris. The orgasms induced with the toy can be quite intense, so be prepared.

4. **A dildo.** A basic penis-shaped dildo is a must. Use it to practice fellatio and to perfect your hand job. It can also be used alone or with a partner to stroke your cervix or to penetrate your vagina. Some are cast from molds of real penises, complete with veins and testicles.

5. **The finger vibrator** is the perfect toy to introduce toys to your male partner. It can be placed on his finger, allowing him to maintain control.

It is, therefore, less threatening for the man who fears that toys will replace him in your life. The vibrations produced are perfect for stimulating your vulva and clitoris. It can also be used to stimulate his penis or perineum.

6. **The Natural Contours vibrator** looks more like a small medical device than a sex toy. Designed by adult filmmaker Candida Royalle, it is sleek, smooth, and perfectly designed to fit along the natural curve of your vulva. The vibrations are gentle and comfortable. It is perfect for the woman who is new to sex toys as well as for the more experienced.

7. **The G-spot vibrator.** This vibrator is easy to detect due to the curve at the top of the shaft. This curve allows the top of the vibrator to press against your G-spot when inserted in your vagina. You can also buy a dildo shaped for G-spot stimulation without the vibration.

8. **The vibrating bullet.** This tiny powerhouse is capable of creating pleasurable sensations for you and your partner. It is made to stimulate your clitoris and fits nicely on top of or between your outer labia.

continued

When bored, you can simply drop the bullet in your panties and sit back and enjoy your private encounter. The bul- 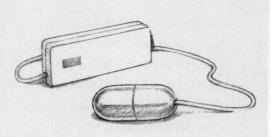 let is also great for partnered sex. Place it against your clitoris while having intercourse or anal sex for increased erotic pleasure.

9. **Strap-on vibrator.** Most women find it difficult to orgasm during intercourse. Well, this vibrator makes it easier to reach climax during intercourse. It has straps that hold it 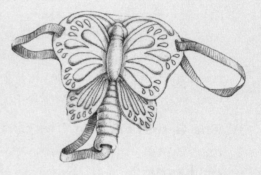 in place against your clitoris while leaving your vagina and anus free for intercourse. It provides just the additional stimulation that you need for ultimate pleasure.

10. **Vibrating cock ring.** He will love you for this one. The stretchable cock ring is placed at the base of his erect penis. The attached vibrating egg should be rotated to the top of the ring. That way, when you have intercourse,

continued

the vibrating egg has direct contact with your clitoris, providing the additional clitoral stimulation that most women need during intercourse. He also feels the vibrations at the base  of his penis and scrotum. To increase clitoral stimulation, assume the woman-on-top position and grind your hips against the egg attachment.

stimulate his nipples, perineum, anus, or penis. Experiment, taking turns to see what works for both of you.

But if he's looking for something a little different from your personal vibrator, you can find toys made just for him.

Cock Rings

As their name suggests, these rings fit over the penis shaft, encircling the base of the penis, or the penis and testicles. They restrict blood flow out of the penis, which keeps it engorged and helps his erection last longer. Rings may be made of plastic, rubber, leather, or metal.

One word of caution: If he's using a cock ring, make sure he doesn't limit blood flow out of the penis for an extended period of time. Most urologists suggest no more than twenty minutes. Prolonged restriction of blood flow may cause damage to his penis. Choose rings that can be adjusted with snaps or ones that are made of stretchy rubber so they can be removed easily (and quickly in case of an emergency). And don't use the ring if it is too tight or causes pain.

Butt Plugs

Essentially small dildos designed to fit and stay in the anus, they have a flared bottom that prevents them from sliding too far up your rectum. You can insert one while participating in oral, vaginal, or manual sex to give your partner an extra shot of stimulation. Never use plugs that are more than 4 inches long; they could cause internal damage.

Penis Sleeves

Made of jelly rubber, cyberskin, or silicone, they slip over the penis and are used for masturbation. Place lubricant in the sleeve prior to inserting the penis for a feel that is similar to the vagina.

More Sex Toys

Anal Beads

As part of foreplay, your partner slowly inserts these beads one by one into your anus; then, at the height of orgasm, he pulls them out, stimulating anal nerve endings.

Swiss Love Ball

This 36-inch inflatable ball can help you give your lovemaking a boost by enabling you to practice some creative positions for intercourse. The ball especially supports positions that involve rocking motions or deeper penetration. It gives a whole new meaning to "We had a ball last night."

16

. . . . .

Adult Amusements: Erotic Games

What else can you add to your sex play to encourage communication, heighten arousal, and explore new ways of finding pleasure? Erotic games can do all that while adding another element of fun to your sex life. One thing I like about games is that you don't have to wait until you're in the bedroom to play them. In fact, you don't even have to be face to face. Imagine you call your lover from work in the morning, start up a subtle, sexy game over the phone. Then you can call or e-mail each other during the day, taking turns turning one another on. By the time you get home, the sexual anticipation is so intense, you're hardly able to get in the door before you're tearing one another's clothes off. Sounds like fun, doesn't it? And, of course, game play can take place immediately before, during, or after sex. The best thing about this game is that, ultimately, both players win.

You can purchase sexy games from sex shops, lingerie stores, catalogs, and the Internet. Or you can create your own games—board games, word games, or whatever your playful mind can devise—something unique that you share only with your lover. Below are some of my favorite games, which you can purchase (see "Resources"), as well as some ideas for sensual games that you can create on your own.

Game Time

Here are some erotic games that will spice things up for you and your partner. You can find these games on-line (see "Resources").

- *52 Weeks of Romance:* Open a black satin bedside bag filled with surprising, adventurous, seductive, scratch-and-reveal cards that suggest lovemaking ideas for you and your mate for the next twelve months.

- *52 Weeks of Naughty Nights:* This game also features the satin bag filled with suggestive scratch-and-reveal cards, but the suggestions are more naughty than nice.

- *The Card Game for Lovers:* Couples select from a deck of fifty-four cards to get ideas for sensual fun and to spark intimate communication. As each card is played, you'll learn more about each other's fantasies and heighten your sexual desire for each other. Ultimately, you may even find you've strengthened your bond.

- *Foreplay: A Game for Lovers:* The perfect game for opening important discussions between intimate partners. Explore each other's thoughts, fantasies, sexual experiences, and desires by rolling the dice and traveling around the board. Lovers learn new foreplay techniques and gain a new understanding of their own bodies as well as their lover's.

❧ *For Lovers Only (Parts I and II):* A couple's sensual action game that enables them to travel the game board by using playing cards, pawns, and dice. This game offers an erotic way for lovers to get acquainted. The object of the game is to keep your clothes on as long as possible.

❧ *Romantic Rendezvous:* A board game with cards designed for couples to promote love, affection, joy, and laughter. Players travel around the board and follow instructions on the various spaces, directing them to perform an intimate act or express feelings or thoughts.

Design Your Own Fun

Use your imagination to design your own personal toys and games. Here are a few suggestions:

❧ **Bull's-eye:** Use your favorite flavored body paint to create a bull's-eye on the part of your body that you think needs special attention. Then give your partner sixty seconds to creatively clear off the bull's-eye by using his or her mouth. Each player gets five chances, but this activity is such a turn-on that you'll likely be making love before the game is over.

❧ **Create your own board game:** Spice up an old board game— you can find them at secondhand and thrift shops—by covering each square with your own personal instructions for sex play (kiss your partner's lips, kiss the area of your partner's choice, massage your partner's breasts, etc. . . .). To play, each person takes turns rolling the dice and then moving his or her game piece the corresponding number of spaces. Of course, you have to follow the instructions that appear on the space where you land, and that will create some healthy sexual tension throughout the game. The first person to complete the board wins and can choose the sex play for the rest of the encounter.

 Pleasure dice: Find some ordinary dice and glue your own arousing instructions on each surface. Use words such as *lick, bite, massage, stroke, tickle, suck,* etc., on one die. On the other one, use words or pictures illustrating body parts: breasts, toes, buttocks, lips, etc. You and your partner take turns rolling the dice and follow the instructions.

 Pleasure dice 2: Another spin on the Dirty Dice concept is to use the numbers on the dice to represent different sexual activities. Assign each number from 2 to 12 to a different sex act. For example, 2 for oral sex, 3 for deep kiss, 4 for perineal massage, 6 for five-minute massage of "sacred spot," etc. Then take turns rolling the dice and performing the sex act that corresponds to the number that you roll.

 Grab bag: Evenly distribute twenty index cards between you and your partner. Then each of you uses your ten cards to vividly describe your favorite sexual experience (with your partner, of course), a favorite fantasy, or an activity that you'd love to try. Next, fold the cards in half, place them in a covered box, and give the box a good shake. One of you selects a card and seductively reads the instructions on it. Then practice making those sensual thoughts a reality; don't stop until you and your partner both get it right. To heighten sexual tension, try selecting the card in the morning before you begin your day, and anticipate bringing its instructions to life later that night. Remember, you've got nineteen more nights of sexual excitement as both you and your partner continue to act out the remaining cards.

∝ *Kama Sutra:* Get an illustrated version of the ancient sex manual and make copies of several different sexual positions. Next fold each piece of paper and place it in a bowl or box. Each day, draw one piece of paper from the box and declare it the position of the day. Enjoy bringing that paper to life and start fantasizing about what positions may come up next.

∝ *Twenty-one:* Shuffle a pack of playing cards and allow each partner to select two cards from the deck. Compute the value of your cards, counting face cards as ten points. The person whose total is closest to twenty-one determines which article of clothing the other player has to remove. The first one to end up naked loses (or wins). Don't have cards? You can play the same game with a pair of dice by allowing the person who rolls the higher number to determine which article of clothing the partner removes.

∝ *Write on:* Here's a game that you can play over several days or weeks. It's especially exciting for couples who are in long-distance relationships or when one partner is traveling. One of you starts the story (or fantasy) by introducing a particular scene. Then, allow your partner to take up where you left off in the story, adding the next paragraph or scene. Then it's your turn to add to the tale. (You can communicate the story via e-mail, mail, telephone, or in person. The only suggestion here is that you actually write down the story that develops so that each of you can keep track of it and look back on it when you're done.) The story ends when you both feel the story is complete and you're ready to act out the script yourselves. The anticipation and excitement created over the course of the story will spill over into a passionate encounter between you and your partner.

17
· · · · ·

The Pleasures of Fantasy

You're at the party of the year. All your friends are there, along with scores of fascinating, lovely people laughing and enjoying themselves. As wonderful as everyone looks all dressed up, you know you stand out. As you cross the room, chatting with this one and sharing a joke with that one, your silk gown skims your body sensuously. The neckline dips low to show smooth, inviting cleavage; the fabric hugs your hips to their best advantage. You've heard men whispering *Who is she? She's gorgeous.* But you have your eyes on your host. He's handsome, successful, athletic; you've also heard he's an astounding lover. You've flirted with him at other social gatherings—lots of innuendo and veiled suggestion—and you'd love to get to know him better—a lot better.

Suddenly, he's standing behind you very, very close, close enough, you hope, to smell your perfume. He's handing you a glass of champagne, and he's whispering in your ear: *I've been watching you all night. You have me absolutely mesmerized. Dance with me?* He takes you in his arms and pulls you close. Your body warms; so does his. You can feel yourself melting. But you feel him swelling with desire for you. He whispers in your ear again: *Let's go somewhere so we can be alone. . . .*

What comes next? You decide. It's your fantasy. For you, the setting might be a hot Hollywood soirée. Or maybe it's a ball in Victorian England. It might end with him taking you to his study, sweeping all the papers off his desk, and making love to you on its mahogany surface. Or calling for his private plane and whisking you off to a tropical island, where you make love on a moonlit beach. Or maybe you'll sneak off to his secret S&M salon, where he'll handcuff you to the bed and have his way with you. Whatever turns you on.

That's the wonderful thing about fantasies. You can be whomever you want, wherever you want, having the best sex of your life with whomever you desire. And it always ends happily ever after, with you satisfied down to your toes.

The good news is that fantasy isn't just a fun mental exercise. It's actually good for your real-life sex life. Research shows that women who engage in fantasy are more likely to have a satisfying sex life. I do believe fantasy can definitely change so-so sex into sensational sex. It can increase your desire, arousal, and pleasure. When you engage in fantasies during sex, it keeps your mind focused on the pleasurable sensations that you are feeling, increasing the chance that you will experience orgasms as well as making them more intense. It's a safe, private, pleasure enhancer and an important part of our sexual expression.

Though most of us don't share our fantasies, most of us have indulged in a fantasy at some point in our lives. And while you may think of fantasy as a woman thing, it's important to realize that men fantasize too; they just do it a little differently. Though it's difficult to generalize (and there are exceptions), men's fantasies tend to be more sexually explicit and focused on the physical act. (They indulge their fantasies in strip clubs and with porn magazines.) Women's fantasies tend to be more emotional and romantic. Perhaps that's why those bodice-ripping romance novels sell so well among female readers. Men more often imagine doing something sexual to their partner, whereas women more often imagine something sexual being done to them.

But we shouldn't generalize. The whole point of fantasy is that you get to do or be whatever you like, whatever turns you on. And I believe every woman should cultivate a rich, exciting sex life in the privacy of her own mind.

Some Popular Female Fantasies

Reliving a Past Sexual Experience

Remembering the intimate details of a pleasurable experience you've had can increase your desire and arousal. The memory need not be of the actual sexual act but can be centered on the romance, intimacy, love, and warm feelings you experienced. Through fantasy, you can make the memory of great sex into a memory of mind-blowing sex.

Sex with Your Partner

Your fantasies don't have to include some tall, romantic stranger. You can relive past encounters or rehearse future ones with your own special guy. You can imagine doing something totally wild and crazy or blissfully romantic and loving with the one you love. The choices are limitless, and it can turn mundane, predictable sex into something exciting. This fantasy is most common in single women, who tend to fantasize about the guy they are currently dating.

Sex with a Different Man

Whereas single women most commonly fantasize about sex with their partners, studies have shown that married women are the ones most likely to fantasize about "another man." Indeed, this fantasy is one of the most common for women. Remember, fantasizing sex with another man does not mean that you want to go out and have an affair with this man. Or that you desire or love your partner less. (And if you're even thinking about feeling guilty, don't. Fantasies of having sex with another partner are just as common in men, so it's entirely possible that your partner has similar fantasies.)

Sex with a Woman

The thought of making love to a woman is quite common among heterosexual women, and homoerotic fantasies do not necessarily mean that you subconsciously desire sex with a woman. Yet many women fear that the fantasy means that they are unsure about their sexual orientation. If you love yourself and celebrate women, it seems only natural that you might have thoughts of sharing an intimate and nurturing experience with another woman. If this is a fantasy that comes to mind, go ahead and explore it. If you can accept this kind of fantasy as normal and common, you may find that it's less threatening than you originally imagined. Then you can give yourself permission to fully enjoy the pleasure of the fantasy.

Sex with More Than One Lover

The thought of being involved in a ménage à trois has always been a favorite fantasy of both men and women. No wonder women enjoy it; imagining yourself desired by two people at the same time can be quite arousing. Imagine many hands, lips, tongues, and private parts pleasuring you at the same time and you pleasuring them right back. Through such a fantasy you can be the center of your own orgy without the risks of disease, injury, or a jealous mate.

Sex in a New Location

Tired of having sex in the same place and the same way? You can have sex anywhere you want. A moonlit beach, on your desk at the office, in the elevator of your apartment building (while the other tenants wait) are all fair game when you are in fantasyland. Imagining having sex on a beach in the Mediterranean can make sex in your own bed that much more exciting.

Oral Sex

Though 75 percent of men and women have had some experience with oral sex, only about a quarter of us practice cunnilingus or fellatio regularly, according to the National Health and Social Life Survey. For many women, the mystique surrounding oral sex—performing it or receiving it—makes it extremely exotic and arousing.

Forced Sex

So-called "rape fantasies" are also common in women, though they usually don't involve the violence and trauma of an actual rape. Though you are coerced to have sex in these fantasies, it is often because the man finds you irresistible and can't control his desire to make passionate love to you. His objective isn't to cause you fear or pain but pleasure. Having this type of fantasy does not mean that you want to be raped. It's especially common among women who feel guilty about consenting to sex. Fantasies about being forced to have sex may absolve some of the feelings of guilt.

Forbidden Act

Being a "naughty" girl can be arousing. Thinking about participating in sexual acts that seem deviant, dangerous, unusual, or wild can be extremely pleasurable in fantasy. Fantasy is a safe way of experiencing something that you would never consider doing in real life. And, again, just because you fantasize about something that is forbidden does not mean you want to actually do it. By indulging in your daydreams, you can satisfy your curiosity in a safe, private way, without causing harm to yourself or others.

Dominating a Man

The thought of totally controlling an attractive hunk who finds you irresistible can be a real turn-on. The feeling of power you get from making him fulfill your every desire is a surefire aphrodisiac. Imagine: Tie him up, place a leash around his neck, make him beg for your love. If you'd never think of being the sexual aggressor in real life, you can certainly enjoy being the dominatrix in your own mind.

Seduction

Imagine: He is someone you can't have: your boss, your best friend's husband. You appear. You are beautiful, perfect, delicious. He is attracted to you immediately. He tries to resist, but the magnetism is just too strong. You are irresistible. He must have you now and damn the consequences!

Sex with a Celebrity

Imagine: Your eyes meet as he walks down the red carpet. He undresses you with his eyes. He hungers for your touch. He can have any woman in the world, but he wants only you.

These are just a few of the directions your fantasies might take. Set aside any judgments, concerns, or fears and let your mind go. What scenarios turn you on? Indulge in the details: how things look, feel, sound, smell. A rich fantasy life is an important part of knowing yourself sexually and deepening your pleasure—in your *real-life* sex life.

Passion and the Pen

Lots of people get enjoyment from reading romance novels and sexy literature. It stands to reason: such books are full of steamy scenes described in vivid detail—the texture of her blouse, the exact shade of his hair, the warmth of the rain, and the heat of their passion. The whole fantasy is laid out before you.

You can take a page from those books when it comes to your own favorite fantasy: Write it down. Don't worry if you're not what you consider a great writer. Prose and punctuation are not important; passion and playfulness are. Have fun. Let yourself focus on your fantasy—really explore what you want to happen in your dream encounter. Writing it down forces you to think it through and allows you to capture every detail.

You can write the story alone or coauthor it with your partner. A woman who attended one of my sex seminars told me she let her husband in on her fantasy. She wrote the first paragraph and then passed it on to her husband to write the next one. They passed it back and forth, adding to the story for the next few days, until they couldn't resist the sexual tension that this exercise created. She said that this exercise alone breathed new life into what had become a boring and unsatisfying sex life with her husband.

Another woman used one of her *actual* sexual encounters as a template for the fantasy she wrote. It began with the anticipation of her first date with her partner, and ended in the backseat of his car in a deserted parking lot. Recalling her most memorable lovemaking experience—and capturing it on

  continued

paper—was a real turn-on for her. In fact, she says that in the process of writing she reached a state of arousal that she hadn't experienced since she entered menopause.

Need to give your literary muse a nudge? The tips below can help you write an erotic, sexually arousing story.

- Choose interesting, sexy "characters." First, remember that this is your fantasy and, in it, you can be whoever you want to be. Forget about how you actually look, where you are, what you do for a living, or what you ordinarily do in bed. Imagine the ideal. The same goes for your partner. Of course, you can make up a totally fictional lover. But you can also imagine sharing your fantasy encounter with your lover. In your fantasy, he can be a little taller, a little leaner, have a little more hair or whatever you desire. And if you write about someone other than your partner, be sure to change the names in your story to protect the innocent— and your relationship with your actual partner.

- Bring your characters to life by writing vivid and complete descriptions of every detail of their physical appearance— hair, eyes, lips, right down to the beads of sweat running down their naked bodies.

- Set the scene. Where is this encounter taking place? Describe the physical surroundings in detail, including the time of day, temperature, scents, textures, sounds. Locations that are exotic or taboo may be particularly arousing.

- Create a scenario that begins hours or even days before the characters actually have sex. Create excitement, curiosity, and anticipation of the events to come later in the story.

continued

ᴑᴼ Describe in detail the emotions that the characters are feeling prior to the physical action. Is it love or lust? Are they curious? Nervous with anticipation?

ᴑᴼ Get detailed about the sex. It's not a full-fledged fantasy if you don't explore the sexual aspect of it thoroughly. Include a complete description of how all of the senses—sights, sounds, tastes, textures, scents—of the characters are being stimulated. Let your imagination guide the characters in their exploration of new, interesting, unusual, erotic sexual techniques.

ᴑᴼ Use arousing terms to describe body parts and sexual activities. Don't hesitate to use colorful, erotic language. And if your "character" wouldn't have a problem "talking dirty," then let her rip.

ᴑᴼ Describe the physical sensations that your characters are experiencing, and their emotional and physical reactions to those sensations.

ᴑᴼ Don't be afraid to put your characters in sexual situations that you, personally, would never have the nerve to experience. It is a fantasy after all.

ᴑᴼ Always give your story a happy ending. All characters should be thoroughly, deliciously satisfied!

18
· · · · ·

Pleasure Diet: Nutrients, Supplements, and Aphrodisiacs

Exciting Edibles

When women ask me about aphrodisiacs, I remind them that the mind is the strongest aphrodisiac there is. Once I've said that, I make the point that what you eat affects your sexuality, from desire to orgasm. That's quite clear when you look at what happens during the sexual process.

First off, I'm not joking when I say that your mind is your best aphrodisiac. The brain releases chemicals that send messages of well-being, motivation, and arousal—the feelings that put you in the mood for making love. These neurochemicals are made from the amino acids found in the protein you eat, so it follows that a protein-rich diet contributes to your sexy feelings.

A major component of the sex hormones testosterone and estrogen, which enhance desire, is fat. A diet rich in essential fatty acids, found in vegetable, nut, and fish oils—is essential for these hormones. The mineral zinc, found in sunflower and pumpkin seeds, mushrooms, and seafood (especially—guess what?—oysters!) also produces a necessary testosterone enzyme.

Once you're aroused and ready, you need long-lasting energy for lots of lovemaking. This is where the carbs come in: the fruits and grains you eat are what give you the energy you need for sexual stamina. To convert these carbs into energy, you'll also need a balance of B vitamins, which will also help you digest those hormone-enhancing fats and brain-powering proteins.

So, in fact, just about everything you eat or drink affects your motivation or desire for sex, your ability to respond to sexual stimulation, and the intensity of your response. If you want to have a truly delicious sex life, make sure to get all the vitamins and minerals you need from eating a healthy mix of various foods: fruits, vegetables, whole grains, and lean protein. That may be all the aphrodisiac you need.

Eating for Maximum Pleasure

Bread and Grains: Carbohydrates for Stamina

Carbohydrates are your body's main source of energy. When you eat simple or complex carbs, they're broken down into the sugar *glucose,* the brain and body's preferred energy source. *Simple carbohydrates* include table sugar, fruit, maple syrup, molasses, and honey as well as processed white-four and white-rice products—foods that are sugary or are quickly broken down into sugar. These foods provide a quick rush of glucose and give a short burst of energy. Eating sugary or starchy foods and drinks can increase your levels of serotonin, the neurochemical that makes you feel relaxed and secure but which may interfere with your ability to perform sexually. (You don't want to be too calm and sleepy for an exciting sex episode.) And filling up on sweets may keep you from eating more nutritious foods—the fuel your body needs to function sexually.

Complex carbohydrates include whole grains, beans, and vegetables— foods that release glucose slowly and give you staying power. These are the better carb option, but which grains are "sexiest"? Some people have touted oats, believe it or not, as a sex-stimulating food because they're said to be mildly stimulating and strengthening to the nervous system; they may also ease depression, so you'll feel more like engaging in sex. Wheat germ and many whole grains are high in vitamin E and an essential component in sperm and sex-hormone production.

Meat, Milk, and Protein

Second only to water in abundance in the body, proteins make up 20 percent of your body weight. Protein manufactures your skin, hair, muscles, and organs. It ensures proper brain function. It's responsible for the growth and repair of all body tissue, and it helps create essential sex hormones. And because proteins help you remain alert and energetic, they're a great source of energy when carbohydrates and fats are in low supply.

Proteins are necessary for all aspects of your sexuality from desire to performance, and if you don't have enough of them in your diet your desire for sex may decrease. The most complete sources of protein are meat, eggs, and dairy products, but you can also find it in whole grains, seeds, nuts, beans, and brewer's yeast.

Fruits and Vegetables: Vitamin Powerhouses

When your mom admonished you to eat your vegetables, she did so because she knew they were full of the vitamins you needed for

Aphrodisiacs: Fact or Fiction

Many people swear by the sex-enhancing effects of a number of foods, but can what you eat really help boost your libido? Here's the lowdown.

Asparagus: *No.* This vegetable earned its reputation as a sexual enhancer because of its phallic shape. But though it is packed with valuable nutrients, there is no truth to the rumors about its sexual prowess.

Carrots: *No.* Carrots, too, earned their reputation because of their long, cylindrical shape, but eating them won't make you sexier. A firm carrot can, however, be a sexual aid in a pinch (if you know what I mean).

Cayenne pepper: *No.* Peppers and curry can cause your heart rate to increase and your body to sweat—and you'll have an urgent desire for relief. All these are physical reactions that you experience during sex—which is probably why hot foods are sometimes equated with sex. It is unlikely, however, that you will feel the urge to merge when your mouth is on fire. And heaven forbid you get some of this stuff in your vagina!

Chocolate: *Yes and no.* Chocolate has long been considered a libido booster—one of the reasons that chocolate is a favorite gift on Valentine's Day. Chocolate contains phenylethylamine, a "feel good" chemical, and caffeine, a stimulant, both of which may put you in the mood for sex. However, you will need to consume a great deal of chocolate to obtain these sex-boosting benefits.

continued

Coffee: *No.* The caffeine in coffee is a stimulant and may give you a temporary energy boost, but it does nothing for sexual desire or pleasure.

Garlic: *No.* In fact, eat too much of it and you risk driving your lover away.

Honey: *Yes.* It's thick, sweet, and delicious and it may even make you feel happy and energetic. Honey also contains boron, a mineral that may increase the production of testosterone, the hormone that is responsible for sexual desire.

Oysters: *Yes and no.* Oysters first earned their reputation because of their sexy feminine shape and texture. But oysters have also been shown to contain lots of zinc, a mineral that's important for the production of testosterone, the hormone of desire.

Wine: *Not really.* Alcohol, in moderation, may make you feel more relaxed and reduce your inhibitions, making it easier to engage in sex. However, it may also make it more difficult for you to become aroused and achieve orgasm.

Raw goat's testicles: *Who knows?* I'd rather be celibate!

In my opinion, the bottom line is this: If you believe that a food or supplement will improve your sex life, it will. After all, your brain is your most powerful aphrodisiac.

growth and health. She probably didn't realize she was giving you good sex advice as well. As essential as vitamins and minerals are for your general health, they are also important for good sexual health.

When you don't consume enough of any particular vitamin, your body may not function as well as it could. We will discuss the sexual effects of the vitamins and minerals that are provided by fruits and veggies later in this chapter.

You'll need two to four servings of fruit and three to five servings of vegetables to supply the required vitamins and minerals.

Water

Did you know that water is an absolute necessity for great sex? Your blood—90 percent water—helps transport nutrients, hormones, and oxygen throughout your body, including your sexual organs. And in order for you to even become interested in sex, you need these nutrients and hormones to reach your brain (itself more than 70 percent water).

To function optimally during sex, your muscles (75 percent water) and your lungs (90 percent water) need adequate hydration. All the body's chemical reactions, including those that produce energy, also require water. When your water intake is low, your ability to perform sexually will suffer. When water is low, your body will have to determine how to ration it. Given a choice between supplying your brain or your vagina with fluid, which do you think your body would choose? If your answer is vagina, close the book now and rush to the nearest source of water for a drink.

Let's think about the most basic sexual act: kissing. If you're going to kiss someone (or enjoy other oral pleasures), you need water to keep your lips soft and moist and to produce the saliva that keeps your mouth from being dry. You want your breath to be reasonably fresh; saliva bathes your mouth to help wash away odor-causing bacteria. (One of the causes of morning breath is the smaller amount of saliva the mouth produces as we sleep.) As you kiss, the production of saliva increases, making your tongue, lips, and mouth soft, warm, and moist. If kissing escalates from mouth-to-mouth to oral sex, a moist mouth acts as a natural lubricant, increasing the pleasure of your partner.

Consider what happens if your water intake is inadequate: Your lips may be dry and chapped from dehydration. Dry mouth causes your breath to be unpleasant and makes the nerves in your mouth less sensitive, thus decreasing your kissing pleasure. And oral sex is more difficult and less pleasurable for the both of you.

Water is also necessary for all other sexual pursuits. As you become aroused, your heart beats faster to transport oxygen and nutrients to your muscles. Blood flow to your vagina and breasts also increases, making them feel full and sensitive. Your vagina becomes moist with secretions that are mostly water. More water is used to moisten the air that is now passing through your lungs at a rapid pace. Your joints are lubricated and cushioned by water, making it easier for you to comfortably assume erotic positions. During sex, your muscles are active and generating heat. To prevent your body from overheating, blood is sent to your skin, and you begin to sweat to help cool your body. And what is sweat but salty water? When you are well hydrated, you're energetic, and your endurance is high. If your fluid intake is low, you will feel tired and sluggish, and even a quickie will drain you of energy. When you are dehydrated, even your libido suffers.

Most women don't drink enough water. To make sure you get enough, drink at least eight 8-ounce cups of water every day.

Vitamins

Having the healthiest sex life possible depends on having the healthiest body possible. That means you've got to take your vitamins or be sure you're getting them in your food. Here's the breakdown on vitamins and how they help your sex life.

Vitamin B₁ (Thiamine)

What it does: Keeps your vagina healthy and your energy levels high.

Get it from: Whole grains, beans, peanuts, wheat germ, eggs, sunflower seeds, and fish.

You should know: Alcohol and birth control pills decrease your levels of vitamin B_1.

Vitamin B₃ (Niacin, Niacinamide)

What it does: Makes sex hormones, improves blood circulation, and increases energy. Ensures proper brain and nervous system functioning. It releases the chemical histamine, important in the production of orgasms.

Get it from: Eggs, fish, peanuts, broccoli, carrots, brewer's yeast, and fortified breads and cereals.

You should know: Inadequate intake of niacin may cause fatigue and depression.

Vitamin B₆ (Pyridoxine)

What it does: Creates dopamine, the neurotransmitter that's key to our desire and enjoyment of sex. Helps form histamine (for orgasms) and aids in the function of your muscles, nerves, and immune system.

Get it from: Eggs, chicken, milk, brewer's yeast, wheat germ, spinach, and bananas.

You should know: Inadequate B_6 intake can cause a decrease in your dopamine levels and adversely affect your libido. Birth control pills decrease pyridoxine.

Folate (Folic Acid)

What it does: Gives you energy and increases the level of histamine, necessary for orgasms.

Get it from: Eggs, green leafy vegetables, beans, oranges, peas, oatmeal, carrots, and pumpkin.

What you should know: All women of childbearing age should take folic acid daily.

Vitamin C (Ascorbic Acid)
What it does: Helps make dopamine and norepinephrine, hormones that strengthen our libido and increase our enjoyment of sex.
Get it from: Citrus fruits, green leafy vegetables, tomatoes, broccoli, and cauliflower.
You should know: Birth control pills can decrease available vitamin C.

Vitamin A
What it does: Keeps your vagina healthy and is needed for the production of sex hormones.
Get it from: Carrots, sweet potatoes, cantaloupe, dark leafy greens, red and yellow peppers.

Minerals

Like vitamins, minerals are essential to optimum health. For great sex, adequate intake of some minerals is a necessity. Some of the most important ones are listed below.

Iodine
What it does: Enables proper functioning of your thyroid gland. If you don't have enough of it, you may experience fatigue and a decreased desire for sex.
Get it from: Iodized salt or sea salt, seafood, sesame seeds, soybeans, and green leafy vegetables. Also sea vegetables such as kelp.

Iron

What it does: Increases energy production and forms hemoglobin, the protein that carries oxygen in the blood. Inadequate iron causes anemia, fatigue, and low energy and can interfere with your ability to function sexually.

Get it from: Eggs, meat, fish, green leafy vegetables, whole grains, lentils, beans, and seeds.

You should know: If you take an iron supplement, combine it with vitamin C or B-complex for complete absorption. Look for iron supplements specially formulated to prevent constipation.

Selenium

What it does: Helps to keep your tissues youthfully elastic (and that's great for sex).

Get it from: Meat and whole grains.

You should know: Inadequate selenium can cause fatigue and lowered immunity to infections.

Zinc

What it does: Gives you a healthy vagina or prostate.

Get it from: Eggs, meat, fish, oysters, sardines, seafood, soybeans, and legumes.

You should know: Inadequate zinc can decrease your sense of smell and taste, and affect your libido, causing fatigue and impotence in men.

Herbs

For centuries the world over, herbs have been used to add a little extra flavor to our sex lives. They have been reputed to affect all aspects of our sexuality including desire, arousal, performance, and enjoyment of sex. Some just make us feel better—more cheerful and energized; less depressed and tired—so we'll be more in the mood for lovemaking.

Many people use herbs because they feel that they are the most natural way to enhance sexuality. But it's important to remember that herbs are strong medicine; they may even be toxic in certain dosages or when combined with other herbs or medications. And, unlike pharmaceuticals, herbs aren't widely regulated or standardized, so one form or brand may be more potent than another. If you plan to take herbs, get professional help from an herbalist or from a medical professional who knows how herbs work. When you purchase packaged herbs, buy them from companies known to provide quality products.

Here, I've listed a few of the herbs best known for their sex-enhancing properties. But what works for one person may not work for you, so if you're planning to go the herbal route, be prepared for some trial and error as you find out which herbs work best for you.

Black cohosh
What it is: A North American plant, traditionally used by Native Americans.
Sex value: Its estrogenlike properties regulate a woman's reproductive system. It increases blood flow to your pelvis, increasing your arousal and response to sexual stimulation.
Added benefits: It relieves anxiety and PMS, both of which can interfere with your ability to relax and enjoy sex. It may relieve menstrual cramps as well as menopausal hot flashes and vaginal dryness.

Chasteberry
What it is: The dried fruit of the chaste tree. Also called Vitex.
Sex value: Despite its name, it's a libido booster. It increases dopamine, the neurotransmitter that increases your sexual desire

and enjoyment, and decreases prolactin, the neurotransmitter that interferes with sexual desire.

Added benefits: It's been used to treat the libido-busting symptoms of premenstrual syndrome (PMS). It may also help regulate your periods. Menopausal women may notice an increase in vaginal moisture, making sex more enjoyable.

Caution: Chasteberry may interact with birth control pills and make them less effective.

Damiana

What it is: A small shrub in the Caribbean and Gulf of Mexico.

Sex value: It is used as a sex tonic for women. For some, it has a soothing, calming effect that helps them to relax; for others, it decreases sexual inhibitions and gives them more energy. It may increase blood flow to your genitals, making it easier for you to achieve orgasm.

Added benefits: May relieve depression, fatigue, and anxiety.

Dong Quai

What it is: Also called "female ginseng," it is a root used in traditional Chinese medicine.

Sex value: It relieves menstrual pain, alleviates PMS symptoms, and makes your periods more regular, all of which contribute to an increase in sexual desire.

Added benefits: Some people find it energizing; it gives them the boost they need for great sex. It also offers some women relief from hot flashes and vaginal dryness, making sex more enjoyable.

Evening Primrose

What it is: The oil of a North American wildflower.

Sex value: Rich in essential fatty acids, it may stimulate the desire for sex.

Added benefits: Helps ease PMS symptoms such as breast tenderness. Decreases menopausal hot flashes and vaginal dryness, making sex more enjoyable.

Fo-ti
What it is: A Chinese herbal medicine, used as a stimulant and tonic.
Sex value: Thought to increase blood flow to the genitals. It increases libido and improves performance.
Added benefit: Makes you stronger, more alert, and energetic.

Fenugreek
What it is: A Mediterranean herb that dates back to ancient Egypt and India as an aphrodisiac.
Sex value: It may decrease cholesterol, which helps keep blood vessels healthy, which, in turn, improves blood flow to the genitals. It may increase your libido and arousal.
Added benefits: Increases vaginal moisture in menopausal women.
Caution: May stimulate contractions, so don't take it if you're pregnant.

Garlic
What it is: A plant used for thousands of years to stir sexual appetite.
Sex value: Garlic improves blood circulation and lowers blood pressure so that you have good blood flow to your genitals. Also boosts energy and stamina, de rigueur for fantastic sex.
Added benefits: Garlic boosts the immune system. Women use it as a natural treatment for yeast infections; it eases the symptoms and decreases the number of recurrences.
Caution: If you're concerned about its pungency, take odorless garlic supplements; they're just as effective.

Ginger

What it is: The spicy root of an Asian plant.

Sex value: Increases arousal by improving blood flow to the genitals. Also gives you added energy and stamina for great sex.

Added benefits: Ginger is good for menstrual cramps and discomfort.

Ginseng

What it is: A root used for thousands of years as an aphrodisiac.

Sex value: For women, it increases the desire for sex, in part because it decreases stress, which kills sexual desire—and boosts the energy and strength that you need to perform.

Added benefits: It helps with menopausal symptoms such as vaginal dryness.

Ginkgo biloba

What it is: The leaf of a North American tree.

Sex value: Increases arousal by improving blood flow to the genitals and brain.

Added benefits: It also helps stem depression, a sexual downer.

Gotu kola

What it is: Leaves of Gotu kola plant.

Sex value: Increases the sex drive in women. Improves sexual arousal and performance by increasing blood flow to the genitals.

Added benefits: It relieves depression and anxiety, and promotes relaxation. It's high in B vitamins, necessary for the extra energy required for sex.

Muira puama

What it is: The root of a Brazilian herb, also called "potency wood."

Sex value: It increases your desire for sex. Increases arousal by increasing blood flow to the genitals. It may increase levels of testosterone, as important to women's sexuality as it is to men's.

Red clover

What it is: A flowering herb.

Sex value: It may increase your desire for sex by alleviating the libido-robbing symptoms of PMS.

Added benefits: May lessen menopause symptoms.

Sarsaparilla

What it is: A Central American vine used in the Caribbean and by Native Americans.

Sex value: It may increase libido in both women and men. May improve energy, sexual performance, and enjoyment of sex.

Saw palmetto

What it is: The berries of a small North American shrub.

Sex value: May increase libido and improve enjoyment of sex.

Added benefits: It may also help relieve menstrual cramps. Many men take it for prostate problems. Native women used it to firm their breasts.

St.-John's Wort

What it is: A shrub found in North America and Europe.

Sex value: It is a mood enhancer that may make sex more appealing and desirable.

Added benefits: Boosts energy levels and may also decrease the frequency of herpes outbreaks.

Yohimbine

What it is: The bark of the African yohimbine tree.

Sex value: It increases levels of norepinephrine, a neurotransmitter that increases libido and sexual enjoyment, as well as blood flow to the genitals. It has been approved by the FDA as a treatment for impotence and is available by prescription.

Caution: Because of the risks of serious side effects, the herb should be used only under the care of a doctor or other knowledgeable provider.

As with any pleasure enhancer, experiment with what you eat, taking note of how your body and mind react. Do you feel more aroused, sexier, more "in the mood"? Taking care of your body and putting yourself on a "diet for pleasure" is a healthy change worth making.

VI

. . . . .

A Lifetime of Pleasure

19
. . . . .

Yes, Yes, Yes, I Do! Sex After Marriage

If there is one fact that every woman needs to know before saying "I do," it's that sex *will* change after marriage. When you're first together, the sexual attraction is intense, sexual desire is at an all-time high, and the sex itself is amazing and passionate. You can't keep your hands off each other. Every waking moment is filled with thoughts and fantasies about your beloved. You end one sexual encounter thinking about the next one. You simply can't get enough.

But as early as the first year of matrimony, the frequency of sex decreases for most couples. And not only do they have less sex, but many also report less pleasure and sexual satisfaction. And, unfortunately, this decline usually continues as the years pass. The truth is, it's normal and natural for the intensity of sex to decline over the course of a long-term relationship. It is simply unrealistic to expect frequent, over-the-top, orgasmic, mind-blowing sex every time.

But what happens to all that passion? Often, after marriage, couples get into a sexual routine. Sex becomes rote and predictable: same time, same place, same position time after time after time. The amount of time you spend kissing and touching each other decreases. Oral sex, which is often so important early in a relationship, becomes an occasional treat. Foreplay lasts for two minutes and a half, and afterplay becomes a cursory peck on the lips, followed by a sound sleep. When this happens, it's easy to see why you wouldn't be salivating about sex.

While some degree of sexual boredom is normal, prolonged sexual boredom can kill marital lust. In the worst cases, when desire decreases, one partner or the other may feel abandoned, unattractive, and unloved. If you're the rejected one, you can start to imagine that your spouse is having an affair or wants a divorce. If you're the one who loses desire, you fear that something is wrong with you or wonder if you've fallen out of love. Either way, when your relationship doesn't measure up to your expectations, you may feel angry, afraid, guilty, or just deeply disappointed. Eventually, you may start avoiding sex altogether.

Before you get depressed, know that it doesn't have to be this way. Some couples, once they marry, have even more frequent, satisfying sex than they did before marriage. Think about it: You no longer have to deal with the stress and drama of dating. You're free of the guilt that might be associated with premarital sex. You may perhaps stop worrying about getting pregnant. In other words, you can start to really relax and enjoy yourself. And, with time and attention, you become more familiar with your spouse's needs and desires, and learn to more completely fulfill them. You can see how the quality of sex could actually improve over time.

Sex Is a Necessity

A good sexual relationship is important in marriage. I like what Schmuley Boteach, the author of *Kosher Sex,* writes: "Sex is not a luxury of marriage, but its most basic necessity." Satisfying sex makes couples feel emotionally closer; it bonds couples and increases their attraction to each other. When sex becomes infrequent, it affects your whole relationship. You may start to feel more distant and begin to drift apart; you find yourself arguing more. You wouldn't think something like sex would be able to destroy a strong, emotionally solid marriage, but sexual dissatisfaction is one of the leading factors cited in divorce.

But great sex doesn't just happen. It needs nurturing. Give it the time and attention that it needs. Check out the tips below to find ways that you and your partner can make sure that you keep the sexual flames burning. If you haven't had great sex in a while, it may be awkward at first. Start with small steps and work your way up to more exotic fare. Keeping your sex life fresh and vibrant takes work, but it's absolutely worth the effort.

Secrets of Sexually Successful Couples

Honestly, when it comes to perking up your sex life, some solutions take almost no effort whatsoever. You don't have to rush out and buy a whole new dominatrix wardrobe or learn every move in the *Kama Sutra.* Remember, sex doesn't start with sex. It can start with making a subtle connection, one that builds into sexual desire. Try something simple and innocent. Touch him, for example. Not sexually. Just put your hand on his arm as you talk to him. You'd be surprised what a thrill this will send him. Once you start to feel more in tune with one another on a basic level, you'll want to find more elaborate ways of sharing your connection.

It's the Simple Things

- Kiss one another good-bye each day before you leave and again when you come home.
- Sleep with your bodies touching. Snuggle into the spoon position: lying on your sides, facing the same direction, touching back to front, buttocks to pelvis. At the very least, hold hands or place your arms around each other.
- Compliment your mate. Tell him how good he looks, how great he smells, how broad his shoulders are, how cute his butt is. Let him know that you still find him attractive. Also compliment him on an achievement at work, a household project completed successfully, or the graceful way he handled a tough situation.
- Spend at least fifteen minutes of every day going over the events of the day with each other. Listen, really listen, to your partner.
- Say "Thank you," even when he does something he's "supposed" to do. Even if he's doing something that's part of his normal routine or family role, it's important that your mate feels appreciated.
- Run errands together. You can talk and catch up in the car on the way to the market, the pharmacy, the hardware store.
- Hold hands. Reach for his hand as you're eating dinner or as you walk out to your car in the morning.
- Snuggle while watching television.
- Practice simple acts of kindness. Cleaning the kitchen, shopping for groceries, and putting the children to bed can help your partner get in the mood. The messages your partner will hear are: "I appreciate you. I care about you." These messages can light the sparks that ignite passion.

Get Out of Your Rut

- Send him a romantic card in the mail, just because.
- Make a list of ten things that would put a smile on your face. Have your partner do the same, then exchange lists. Each day, choose one thing from your partner's list and make it happen.
- Place a love note in his briefcase, pocket, or car. It'll give him a little boost when he discovers it later.
- Once a day, kiss for ten seconds without stopping.
- Go on dates the way you did when you were first getting to know each other. Make this time sacred and reserve it for the two of you, alone. Talk, laugh, get to know each other better. Focus on each other.
- Visit a comedy club or watch a funny movie. Laughing relieves stress and increases intimacy.
- Wake him up in the morning with a gentle kiss . . . down there.

Think Sexy

- Engage in verbal foreplay. Call him at work and tell him you can't wait for him to come home. Tell him how much you want him.
- Change locations for sex. Having sex in a different place helps you to see each other as lovers rather than as spouses or parents. Send the kids to Grandma's and do it on the living-room floor. Or come home for a lunchtime quickie on the kitchen table.
- Check into a hotel that rents by the hour. The knowing look of the hotel clerk will be arousing. (Take along a set of sheets or a blanket for clean fun.)
- Be creative. For the next two months, commit to trying something new once a week: a new position, technique, or location. The change will bring new energy into your sex life.
- Try morning sex. Your man's testosterone peaks in the morning, and he may often wake up with an erection. Wake up a little ear-

Dr. Hil says:

- ☙ Never go to bed angry. Resolve your conflicts before you turn in for the night, and do it outside the bedroom. Your bedroom is your sanctuary.

- ☙ Reserve your bedroom for sleep and sex. Move the television, papers from work, even books and other distractions to another room.

- ☙ Take a vacation away from the kids once a year. Plan a romantic getaway that enables you to concentrate only on one another. Leave all concern for domestic responsibilities, job, and career behind.

- ☙ Have sex even if you don't have the desire. Even obligation sex, make-up sex, celebratory sex, and sex when you are tired or otherwise less inclined, keep the juices and love chemicals flowing. The more you do it, the more you will want it.

- ☙ Make sex a priority. Plan for it even if you have to make an appointment for it in your date book or PDA. Then look forward to it every time you check your schedule.

- ☙ Tell him that you love him, and don't assume that he knows or doesn't need to hear it again and again. Verbal reassurances of love are as important to men as they are to women. Feeling loved and cared for can be such a great turn-on.

lier and take advantage of that. (If you avoid sex in the morning because you don't feel fresh, get up a little earlier and freshen up before sliding back into bed naked.)

- ☙ Keep him guessing. Touch or kiss a part of his body that you

As Time Goes By: Things you must always remember about your man

- He needs intimate foreplay as much as you do. Touching, hugging, caressing, snuggling your partner may be just what he needs to increase desire.
- He doesn't intuitively know what turns you on. Talk to him: communicate your needs and desires. Be clear, specific, and gentle. Don't let it come across as a criticism.
- He doesn't want to initiate sex all the time. Take the lead and ask him for sex sometimes. He needs to know that you desire him.
- Men are from Venus, too. He needs to feel physically close to develop an emotional connection, but he also needs to feel appreciated, loved, and accepted.

never kissed before. Surprise him in the shower in the morning. Introduce a new toy. Greet him at the door nude.
- Become an expert at extragenital sex. Learn to give good oral or manual sex. (See chapters 8 and 9 for lots of tips and tricks.) Then take turns pleasuring each other as a precursor to intercourse or as its own exciting sexual activity.

Keep in mind that just as your sexual pleasure is your own responsibility—something to claim, commit to, and continue to improve upon—so is the health of your sexual relationship over the years. What you put in affects what you'll get out and how much true pleasure you can experience together for a lifetime.

20
. . . . .

Passion and Parenthood

Having a baby can be the most thrilling experience of your life; you and your spouse will be more elated than you can imagine. But once you get that little bundle home and the initial excitement wears off, it will soon become apparent how much stress this happy addition is adding to your relationship. Unfortunately, few couples are prepared for the life-changing effects of parenthood, and no one seems to talk about the havoc a baby can wreak on your sex life.

If you find yourself completely without desire for sex, understand that you're not alone and you have perfectly good reasons for your feelings:

You're healing. Depending upon whether you had a vaginal delivery or a Cesarean, it can take several weeks to several months for you to get back to normal physically. Don't try to engage in sex before you're fully healed and have your doctor or midwife's go-ahead. But you may be able to enjoy manual sex or other sexual stimulation before you're okayed for intercourse.

Your breasts aren't your own. Once a sensual and important component of your sexual life, if you are breast-feeding, they are now full-time milk producers. Some women won't let their partner anywhere near their breasts while they're nursing; others are less squeamish. And, while your new bustiness is appealing, some men are afraid of being squirted by breast milk. This is an area you'll have to navigate together. Many couples find a healthy middle ground.

Your hormones are haywire. You probably became accustomed to the hormone fluctuations of pregnancy; don't forget that those hormones are still raging and trying to adjust themselves after you give birth. You may find that you're moody, weepy, or tense, and your sex drive may be at an all-time low. Be gentle with yourself and stay in communication with your husband. Things should calm down in a few weeks.

You're exhausted. Caring for a new baby—or for an older one, for that matter—leads to both physical and emotional fatigue. Feeding, diapering, changing, comforting becomes a never-ending cycle during the day. Then you're up and down all night doing the same thing. Sleep may be more appealing than lovemaking. Take naps with your baby during the day, so that you're a little more energetic at night. Learn the art of the quickie so you can get a little love before the baby wakes up. When you do make love, choose positions that are easy for you. (Let him do the work.)

Your sexual self-esteem and self-image change. Your body has changed. Your priorities have shifted from being part of a couple to being responsible for a child. You may begin to see yourself more as a mother than a sexy, sensual woman. Don't let yourself lapse into the frumpy mom. Make sure there's at least one sexy outfit in your wardrobe. Stretchy pants and a low-cut blouse take advantage of your new curves, and they're comfortable and practical for a new mom. Take the baby for vigorous strolls, and take advantage of all the bending and lifting of the little one to get yourself back into shape. You'll feel better about your body and are more likely to want sex.

You're pulled in new directions. At the end of the day, sex becomes just one more thing you have to do for someone else. You may resent your husband's requests for sex and attention; he may feel abandoned, hurt, and angry. Talk it out: tell him how you feel and really listen to his feelings. Sometimes just being able to communicate is a good first step toward renewing your sex life.

You're afraid you might wake the baby. Your baby may be within earshot so that you can hear her in the night. But if you can hear her, you figure she can hear you, which may make you squeamish about embarking on a passionate lovemaking session. And often parents have their infants in the same room—even in the same bed—which certainly puts a damper on sex. Instead of seeing this as a limitation, use it as an opportunity to put some excitement into your sex life. Slip out of the bedroom and make love on the couch, in the kitchen, or on the floor of another room.

Though it's understandable that you may not be at your sexiest with a baby in the house, don't let your sex life fall by the wayside. Without attention and planning, your sex life can wane, and you'd be surprised at how quickly you and your partner begin to drift apart. (And caring for your little one is that much harder if you and he aren't clicking.) Here are a few tips for keeping it together as a couple when there are three (or more) of you.

- Make your sex life a priority.
- Put a lock on your bedroom door to prevent intrusions on your intimate time.
- Keep your bedroom as your private sanctuary. Don't allow the baby or your older children to sleep in your bed.
- Sneak a quickie in the bathroom.
- Arrange for a babysitter once a week so you can spend intimate time with your spouse. The two of you can go out; better yet, have the sitter take the little ones to a movie, the zoo, or the park while you and your man stay home. If you can't afford a babysitter, form a babysitting co-op with other moms. Each week one of the mothers will agree to take all of the children while the others have private time with their spouses.
- Remember to take a few hours every week for "me" time. Don't forget that you are also important and need nurturing. Feeling good about yourself is essential to having a satisfying sex life.

21

. . . . .

Sex After Fifty

Sex after fifty can and should be the best of your life. Sure, it isn't the same that it was when you were thirty, but *different* does not have to mean less satisfying. With age comes confidence and self-awareness, both of which are necessary for satisfying sex. At fifty you can be flirtatious, foxy, fabulous, and frisky, and no one dare say anything about it.

I call the fifties the "It's all about me" decade. You've taken care of everyone else's needs before your own. Now it is time to take care of yourself and make sure that you experience all of the pleasures that life has to offer, and that includes sexual pleasures. Accept pleasure. In fact, search for it and embrace it.

Let's look at ways that you can make sure that your sex life remains satisfying in your fifties and beyond.

Become a CAT

Members of the CAT Society:

- ❧ Are **C**onfident: "I am a sensational, sexy, sensuous woman."
- ❧ Have **A**ttitude: "I deserve sexual pleasure, and I won't accept anything less."
- ❧ Are **T**echnically savvy: "I know how to bring pleasure to myself and my partner."

Membership is limited to women over fifty who have learned to celebrate their sexuality and embrace pleasure. Form your own chapter.

Take Care of Your Vagina

As you age, your vagina may become more dry. That's because your ovaries produce less estrogen. When estrogen is low, the blood supply to your vagina and clitoris may decrease, causing less arousal and vaginal dryness. But it doesn't have to be that way.

To keep your vagina moist and plush, you should remain sexually active as you age. That means having sex with a partner regularly or, if you don't have a partner, masturbating. Stimulating your clitoris and labia alone will keep the juices flowing and decrease dryness. But to protect the length and width of your vagina, you need to stimulate the vaginal tissue directly. At least once a week you should use a well-lubricated dildo, vibrator, or two or three fingers to massage your vagina for at least fifteen to twenty minutes. Doing so will prevent your vagina from becoming smaller. And it can be a lot of fun.

It may take longer for you to lubricate, so take your time during foreplay. Kiss, stroke, and massage each other until your vagina lets you know that the time is right for penetration. If your partner is also over fifty, chances are good that he also needs the extra time to become erect (unless, of course, he has popped the little blue pill).

This is a good time to expand your definition of sex. Lubrication is less important for oral sex and is almost guaranteed to increase your arousal. Stimulating each other manually (with a lubricant) can be immensely pleasurable.

Practice your Kegel exercises every day (see page 52 for instructions). Exercising your PC muscle will increase the blood flow to your pelvis.

If you already find that your vagina is dry and sex is painful, there are several options. The first is to use a water-based lubricant every time you have sex. Massage a generous amount of the lube on your vulva and the entrance to your vagina. Use your fingers or those of your partner to push more lube into your vagina. Then massage lube on his penis. Two slippery surfaces sliding against each other will decrease friction and pain, and increase your pleasure.

If you still experience pain, you should consider estrogen replacement therapy. If you do not want to take systemic hormones, you can try local vaginal estrogen. The estrogen modalities products listed below may be effective in replenishing the vagina with moisture needed to keep it soft and plump.

    Estrogen cream: I recommend that you use a small amount every day until your vagina is moist and you are no longer having pain. Then you can decrease the frequency of application. Take a bean-sized amount of the cream on your finger and massage into the opening and along the length of your vagina. Spend at least three minutes on the massage. You can use larger amounts of the cream but will also need to add progestin hormone to protect your endometrium from endometrial cancer.

- *Estring* is a soft flexible ring that contains estrogen hormone. The ring is placed in your vagina, where it releases a low steady dose of estrogen for three months.
- *Vagifem* is a small tablet that contains estrogen hormone. The tablet is inserted into your vagina twice a week.

Take Care of Your Clitoris

As you age, your clitoris may also lose some of its sensitivity, and as a result it may take longer for you to orgasm. Again, remaining sexually active will prevent many of the changes in your clitoris.

A medical device, the *Eros therapy device,* may also help increase your sensitivity. This small, handheld device is applied to your clitoris and creates a gentle suction that increases the blood flow to your clitoris. When used three to four times a week, some women found that the intensity of their orgasms increased. The Eros device must be prescribed by a doctor.

Some women have found that *testosterone cream or gel,* when applied to the clitoris, increased their sensitivity and made orgasms more intense. Testosterone therapy requires a prescription from your doctor.

Include *vibrators* in your sex play. Vibrators deliver intense stimulation that many women need as they enter, or after, menopause.

Boost Your Desire

As we age, most of us will notice a decrease in our desire. A loss of desire for sex may be caused by medications, relationship problems, stress, or fatigue. Your libido may also be affected by the natural decrease in testosterone hormone that comes with age. Testosterone

The Little Blue Pill

At some point in every man's life, he will experience a problem getting or maintaining an erection. And as men age, it will become more frequent. For some couples, this can be devastating; for others, the change in the frequency of sex is hardly missed. So what happens when he comes home with a prescription for Viagra, Cialis, or Levitra, medications to help him produce erections?

Well, if the two of you have missed the days when erections were easy and frequent, the pill can be a lifesaver. Take a pill, wait an hour, and then get busy. It can mean the return of an active and satisfying sex life. Or it can mean rushed, mechanical sex that appears to be without emotion. Foreplay may be curtailed in the rush to put the new firm erection to good use. And if you were secretly relieved when his lack of erections gave you an easy excuse to avoid sex, his newfound sexual potency may be irritating—even upsetting.

Sex should always be mutually pleasurable and satisfying. Like all aspects of sex, when it comes to drugs that enhance erections, communication is key. You and your partner must have a discussion about the medication, and Viagra should not be consumed until both of you have agreed that drug-induced sex is on the agenda. To enhance the sexual experience for both of you, sex should begin immediately after the pill has been taken. That means that you have a full hour of foreplay— kissing, hugging, sweet talking, and emotionally connecting to each other—before intercourse (or other sexual activity) begins.

continued

It is important to keep in mind that a firm erection is not necessary for sexual pleasure. Cuddling, caressing, oral and manual stimulation of each other's bodies can provide wonderful physical sensations. The intimacy that you share can also be emotionally and spiritually satisfying.

can be replaced and may be just what you need to get your libido back on track. Testosterone must be prescribed by your doctor.

You can also boost your desire by trying new sexual techniques and making sex more exciting. So be adventurous, and discover what feels good.

Step Outside the Box

Many women over fifty will find themselves without a partner. That doesn't mean that you should give up sex. Be willing to step outside your box. Start a relationship with a man of a different race or ethnicity, or a younger man. Be willing to look at men you would not ordinarily have considered. If you've ever been curious, this may be the time to start a relationship with a woman. It is also perfectly fine to decide that you do not want to be sexual with a partner. Keeping your mind, and your options, open is a key to understanding what you really want.

Create Pleasure for Yourself and on Your Own Terms

Make time for yourself. Set aside several hours a week for personal pleasures. Get a massage, manicure, pedicure, or facial. Take yourself out to lunch or a movie. Journal every day. Take a walk alone. Go skinny-dipping. Go ahead: Live a little! Being good to yourself is the essential foundation for a sex life that satisfies at *any* age.

22
. . . . .

Some Reminders About Safer Sex

Birth Control

When it comes to sexual health, what is absolutely the sexiest thing in the world? Knowing that you'll walk away from your lovemaking session tingling with satisfaction and certain you aren't pregnant (if that isn't what you desire) and don't have a disease.

When you ask people what's sexy, birth control is not usually the first thing on the list. It should be. The best sex happens when you are relaxed, and you can't truly loosen up if you're concerned about sexually transmitted infections and unwanted pregnancy. Nothing will make you tense like nagging questions in the back of your mind: *Why didn't I bring my diaphragm? I wonder if I'm ovulating? Was that some kind of wart I noticed on his penis?* Good, effective contraception allows you to focus on the pleasure of sex rather than on potential negative consequences.

Fortunately, your birth control options are many. Choose an effective yet comfortable contraceptive to allow yourself and your partner the freedom to fully focus on pleasuring each other. The following list is designed to help you choose a contraceptive plan that will work for you. These methods require little or no work on your part, and protection is long-term.

Convenient Methods

Depo-Provera

How it works: A prescription injection, also known as "the shot," containing a progestin hormone that is given every three months at your doctor's office. Depo-Provera prevents ovulation and changes the cervical mucus and lining of your uterus to prevent pregnancy.

What you should know: Depo-Provera has few side effects. The most common complaint is spotting or irregular bleeding, which typically subsides after the first year. Over time, you can expect to have no periods at all while using this method, and it could take several months for your cycle to return once you discontinue Depo-Provera.

Depo-Provera, which is more than 99 percent effective, does not protect against STIs.

Intrauterine Device (IUD)

How it works: An IUD is a small, thin device that is placed in your uterus by a healthcare provider to prevent pregnancy. There are two types of IUDs: The T-shaped Copper-T IUD (Paragard) is a device that prevents his sperm from fertilizing your egg. It provides up to ten years of protection. The Mirena IUD is made of plastic and works by releasing a progesterone-type hormone in continuous low doses. It provides five years of protection.

What you should know: The IUD is 99 percent effective and is very safe. It can be easily inserted and removed by a doctor, and patients can enjoy long-term protection that may be trouble-free.

On the flip side, IUDs do not protect you against sexually transmitted infections, so you must also use condoms if you're not in a mutually monogamous relationship.

NuvaRing

How it works: You insert a soft plastic ring inside the vaginal canal like a diaphragm, but it remains in place for three weeks. While inside, it releases a steady dose of estrogen and progestin to prevent the release of an egg and reduce the mobility of sperm. The ring contains the same hormones as birth control pills. After the twenty-one days, the ring is removed for one week. Then you insert a new ring.

What you should know: The ring also doesn't offer any protection against STIs. The NuvaRing is 99 percent effective.

Ortho Evra

How it works: The small, thin patch releases a continuous dose of estrogen and progestin, which are absorbed through the skin, to prevent ovulation and thicken the cervical mucus. These hormones are the same ones present in birth control pills. Patches are changed once a week for three weeks. Users do not wear a patch on the fourth week.

What you should know: You can place them anywhere that makes you feel comfortable, including your outer upper arm, butt, or stomach. The patches stay in place during physical activity, and the once-a-week dosing is easy to remember. They are 99 percent effective.

The risks and side effects are the same as those of the birth control pill. In addition, the patch may cause skin irritation in some women and does not protect against STIs. Not recommended for women who weigh more than 190 pounds.

Sterilization

How it works: Sterilization is a permanent form of birth control. In women, doctors perform a surgical procedure called a tubal ligation to block the fallopian tubes and permanently prevent sperm from accessing the egg. When you "tie your tubes," doctors burn, cut, tie, or block them. A new apparatus, Essure, is a small, soft, metal device that is placed in the fallopian tube by way of the vagina. This nonsurgical procedure causes your body to form scar tissue around the device, blocking your tubes so eggs can't pass through them.

In men, doctors perform sterilization, or a *vasectomy,* by blocking the tube that carries sperm. The procedure can be done in a doctor's office or an ambulatory surgical center.

What you should know: Both a tubal ligation and a vasectomy are permanent and very difficult to reverse. Neither is a viable option for young people who may want to have children in the future. Sterilization does not provide protection against sexually transmitted infections.

Hormone-free Birth Control Methods

Consider the following barrier methods of protection if you're concerned about using contraceptives that release hormones to prevent pregnancy. Just remember, use of the following methods requires you to plan properly so they don't interrupt your sex play.

Diaphragm

How it works: Before sex, apply spermicide inside the dome of the diaphragm. Then place the soft dome-shaped latex cup securely in your vagina so it completely covers your cervix and blocks his sperm. Diaphragms must be fit by a healthcare provider.

What you should know: To prevent pregnancy, your diaphragm needs to remain in place for at least six hours after sex. It can remain in place for up to twenty-four hours.

If you use the diaphragm every time you have sex, it's 94 percent effective. Although barrier methods generally do not protect against STIs, your risk of contracting gonorrhea and chlamydia are decreased.

Cervical Cap

How it works: Before sex, you place this small latex cup over your cervix to prevent sperm from reaching your uterus. Cervical caps come in different sizes and must be fitted by a physician or nurse practitioner.

What you should know: For effectiveness, a cervical cap has to remain in place for eight hours after sex. It can remain in place for up to forty-eight hours, allowing sexual spontaneity while it is in place. When used consistently, the Prentif cervical cap is 91 percent effective in women who have never had children but drops to 74 percent for women who have given birth. The cap is not recommended for women who have poor vaginal muscle tone, cervical inflammation, a current reproductive tract infection, or any type of vaginal bleeding. Using a cap may decrease your risks of gonorrhea and chlamydia.

FemCap

How it works: FemCap is a hat-shaped silicone rubber cap that is placed in your vagina before sex. It covers the cervix, preventing sperm from entering your uterus, and has a strap for easy removal.

What you should know: FemCap must remain in place for six hours after sex but can be worn for up to forty-eight hours. You can also use it during your period to allow comfortable sex play. It must be fitted by a healthcare practitioner.

The effectiveness rate is between 71 and 86 percent. Using FemCap may decrease your risk of gonorrhea and chlamydia.

Lea's Shield

How it works: You place this dome-shaped disc, made of silicone rubber, in your vagina before sex. It operates by creating a suction that traps air between the shield and your cervix. The shield covers your cervix and blocks sperm from entering your uterus. Like the FemCap, the shield has a strap for removal. Since one-size-fits-all, no fitting is necessary, but you still need a prescription from a physician.

What you should know: You must leave the shield in place for eight hours after intercourse to prevent pregnancy. It can be worn for up to forty-eight hours. The shield, which may decrease your risk of gonorrhea and chlamydia, is approximately 85 percent effective in preventing pregnancy.

Condoms

How it works: The male condom is a sheath that covers the penis and catches the sperm, preventing it from entering your uterus. For full effectiveness, condoms must be placed on the penis at the beginning of intercourse and should be used every time that you have sex. The Reality female condom is a soft plastic pouch that is placed inside the vagina before sex. It also prevents sperm from entering the uterus.

What you should know: If used correctly, the Reality female condom is 95 percent effective in safeguarding against pregnancy. It also protects you from many sexually transmitted infections, including HIV. All male condoms—latex, polyurethane, and natural lambskin—are 98 percent effective against pregnancy. Only latex and polyurethane condoms protect against HIV infections. Overall, condoms are the best method we have available to prevent the transmission of sexually transmitted infections.

Other Methods

Abstinence

How it works: Depending on personal preference, this can mean saying "No" to anything sexual or avoiding only vaginal intercourse. True abstinence, however, safeguards you from a potential pregnancy and sexually transmitted infections because it requires that you avoid vaginal intercourse, anal intercourse, or any other act that might put you in contact with his sperm.

What you should know: Abstinence is the only truly 100 percent effective means of preventing pregnancy and sexually transmitted infections.

Birth control pills

How they work: Oral contraceptives contain the hormones estrogen and progestin. The most common type, the combined synthetic pill, suppresses ovulation. The progestin-only variety, the mini pill, alters the cervical mucus to make it difficult for the sperm to enter the uterus.

What you should know: The Pill is well tolerated by most women, but some complain of side effects such as weight gain, breast tenderness, moodiness, vaginal dryness, and a decreased sex drive. Often, changing the prescription takes care of the problem. Users of the mini pill tend to have fewer side effects.

Emergency Contraception

No matter how careful you are, occasionally accidents do happen. The condom breaks, you discover a hole in your diaphragm *after* sex, or you may simply forget to take your pill. When those things occur, you do have options.

Emergency contraception could prevent pregnancy if you think your birth control has failed or if you've had unprotected sex. The "morning-after pill," as it's popularly called, is about 75 to 89 percent effective and should be taken within five days of unprotected intercourse. (It is most effective if taken within three days of unprotected sex.) Plan B, two pills containing only progestin hormone, is the only medication designed to prevent pregnancy after unprotected sex. High doses of birth control pills, as prescribed by your doctor, may also be effective. Another option, a copper-containing IUD, can also prevent fertilization. If inserted within five days of unprotected sex, it could reduce your risk of pregnancy by 99 percent.

The Pill, which does not protect against sexually transmitted infections, is 99 percent effective in preventing pregnancy when taken properly.

Sexually Transmitted Infections

Now that you've read through all the sexy, exciting things you can do to improve your love life, you're probably eager to start having some serious fun. I say go for it. But not before you stop long enough to give some serious thought to safer sex.

It's important to learn as much as you can about sexually transmitted infections and how to prevent them. It starts before you have sex of any kind, with anyone. The good news is that, with the wide variety of fun safety gear that's available, there is no reason not to have safer, healthy, wild, fabulous sex every time.

STIs: You Need to Know

Bacterial Vaginosis

Bacterial vaginosis (BV), sometimes characterized by vaginal irritation and discharge, results from a change in the different types of bacteria in the vagina. Although BV isn't always due to intercourse, sexually active women run a higher risk of developing the condition.

How do I know if I have it? Your gynecologist can determine if you have BV by performing a pelvic exam, testing your vaginal secretions, and examining a sample of your vaginal tissue under a microscope. Although many women have no symptoms, the most common ones include vaginal discharge and a strong, unpleasant vaginal odor.

How is it treated? BV is treated with antimicrobial creams. Condoms may reduce the risk of developing BV.

Chancroid

Chancroid is a condition caused by a bacterium, *Hemophilus ducreyi*. It is uncommon in the United States.

How do I know if I have it? You might notice one or several painful ulcers on the opening of your vagina or vulva. Also, you might have swollen lymph nodes (glands) where your hips and mons meet. Symptoms occur approximately seven days after contact. Your doctor will diagnose you by performing special cultures.

How is it treated? Chancroid can be treated with antibiotics.

Chlamydia

Chlamydia is caused by an organism called *Chlamydia trachomatis*. It is the most common sexually transmitted infection in the United States. Most women infected with chlamydia do not have symptoms. A few women have a heavy yellow discharge from the vagina.

How do I know if I have it? The diagnosis is made when your doctor performs a culture. You should specifically ask to be tested for chlamydia as it may not be part of your routine exam. Chlamydia may infect your cervix, anus, throat, and urethra.

How is it treated? Both partners must be treated with antibiotics. Follow-up testing should occur three or four months after treatment. If untreated, chlamydia may cause pelvic infections, damage to your fallopian tubes, ectopic pregnancy, and infertility. Condoms will decrease your risk of infection as will the other barrier methods of birth control.

Gonorrhea

Gonorrhea is caused by a bacterium called *Neisseria gonorrhea*. It is the second most common sexually transmitted infection in the United States.

How do I know if I have it? Most women infected with gonorrhea do not have symptoms. Those with symptoms may notice a heavy yellow discharge, burning when urinating, or abnormal menstrual periods. Gonorrhea can affect your anus, throat, cervix, and urethra.

How is it treated? The diagnosis is made when your doctor performs a culture of any of the affected areas, and the infection is treated with antibiotics. Since chlamydia often accompanies gonorrhea, you and your partner should be treated for both infections. If left untreated, gonorrhea may cause pelvic infections and infertility. Using condoms and other barrier methods of birth control may decrease the risk of infection.

Hepatitis

Hepatitis B infection is caused by the hepatitis B virus (HBV), which is spread through semen, blood, urine, and saliva. HBV, however, can be prevented with vaccination. The sexual transmission of the hepatitis A virus (HAV) and hepatitis C virus (HCV) is less common.

How do I know if I have it? Many people with hepatits have no symptoms. Those with symptoms may have headaches, fever, extreme fatigue, nausea, vomiting, lack of appetite, and tenderness in the abdomen. The condition is diagnosed by a blood test.

How is it treated? There is no treatment for hepatitis infection; however, your immune system will most likely fight the infection successfully. Sexually active women should get the vaccine to protect from possible infection.

Herpes

Genital herpes infections are caused by the herpes simplex virus types 1 and 2. Herpes type 1 typically infects your mouth but can be spread to your genitals. Herpes type 2 more typically infects the genitals. It is estimated that one in four Americans are infected with genital herpes. Most women and men infected with herpes are not aware that they are infected yet are able to transmit the virus to others.

How do I know if I have it? If you do have symptoms, you may notice a sore, blisters, or an ulcer on your vagina or vulva. The lesions could appear as a cluster of blisters or a tiny spot the size of a pinhead. The lesions may be painful or itch and can last for weeks or only for a few days. The diagnosis is made when your doctor performs a culture or a blood test looking for antibodies to the virus.

How is it treated? There is no cure for herpes, and the virus will remain in your body. But there are antiviral medications that can treat your symptoms. The FDA has approved using one of the antiviral medications, Valtrex, or valacyclovir, on a daily basis to decrease your own outbreaks and decrease the risk that you will pass the virus to your sexual partner. If you have an outbreak, you should refrain from sexual activity with another person. Using condoms may decrease the spread of the virus but will not eliminate the risk completely because infected lesions can exist in areas that are not covered by a condom.

HIV (Human Immunodeficiency Virus)

HIV infection is caused by the human immunodeficiency virus, which attacks your immune system and, eventually, causes AIDS. The virus is transmitted through direct contact with blood, semen, vaginal secretions, breast milk, and, to a smaller degree, saliva. The greatest risk of transmission is with anal intercourse. But the virus can also be transmitted by vaginal sex and, to a lesser degree, oral

Sexy Safety Aids

The Reality female condom. Inserted in your vagina, this condom lets you take charge of your protection. Since the polyurethane sheath covers your vagina and most of your vulva, you have more protection from sexually transmitted infections like herpes, genital warts, and HIV.

Dental dam and plastic wrap. Although dental dams are traditionally used by dentists, these small latex squares can also protect you from STIs when you or your partner perform oral sex on the vagina or anus. Hold the squares in place to prevent exposure to lesions as well as anal or vaginal secretions. You can buy dental dams in different sizes and flavors for variety. Also, add a water-based lubricant on the side of the dam that touches the skin for heightened pleasure. Another option is the Glyde dam, a thinner alternative that has FDA approval. And if you need to go thinner, use plastic wrap right from your kitchen cabinet.

Finger cots. As its name implies, these are thimblelike latex covers that provide a barrier when your partner inserts his finger in your vagina. You can also use them if you want to insert your finger in his anus. Just in case you have an abrasion, cut, or lesion, finger cots minimize your chances of catching infections like HIV, warts, herpes, and hepatitis B and C.

Condom Care

Use latex and polyurethane condoms to protect against HIV infections. Also, choose condoms that do not contain nonoxynol-9. This spermicide may cause swelling of your vagina during vaginal intercourse, and damage your anus and rectum during anal intercourse, increasing the risk of transmission of HIV.

sex. Your risk of contracting HIV from an infected partner is increased if you have other sexually transmitted infections.

How do I know if I have it? Two to four weeks after exposure to HIV, 70 percent of HIV-infected people will develop flulike symptoms in the early phase of the infection. But many will not have any symptoms. More advanced symptoms include unexplained rapid weight loss, diarrhea, lack of appetite, fevers, night sweats, and headaches. The diagnosis is made by blood tests used to detect the HIV antibody. It could take up to six months after exposure before you actually test positive.

How is it treated? There is no cure for HIV, but there are retroviral medications that can delay the progression of AIDS, a fatal disease. Using latex or polyurethane condoms every time you have sex will reduce your risk of contracting HIV.

HPV (Human Papilloma Virus)
Human papilloma virus infection may cause either genital warts or an abnormal Pap smear. Virtually all cases of cervical cancer are

How to Use a Condom

A condom should always be put on before any contact with your genitals, anus, or mouth. The clear fluid that is released from the penis when it becomes erect and before ejaculating may contain bacteria and viruses that cause sexually transmitted infections.

Unwrap the condom and slide it down the shaft of the penis. Hold the tip of the condom as you roll it down. Apply water-based lubricant to the surface of the condom to decrease the chance of breakage. Immediately after ejaculation, hold the base of the condom to prevent leakage of semen and remove the penis from your vagina. Unroll the condom and discard. (Find sensual variations for putting a condom on, page 296.)

caused by HPV. There are hundreds of different types of human papilloma virus. Fortunately most HPV infections are benign and cause nothing more than genital warts. It has been estimated that more than 80 percent of sexually active women will become infected with HPV during their life spans.

How do I know if I have it? If you're infected with HPV, you may develop warts on your vulva or vagina that may or may not cause symptoms. When the virus affects your cervix, you may get an abnormal Pap smear. Most of these infections will spontaneously resolve themselves within a year. In a small number of cases, the virus will persist and cause cervical cancer or a lesion that may lead to cervical cancer over time. If you have an abnormal Pap smear, your doctor will follow you closely and may recommend further studies to evaluate your cervix. It's important to see your doctor regularly until all signs of infection have resolved. A new test that detects the DNA of the human papilloma virus is now available. If you are over thirty, ask your doctor for an HPV DNA test.

Condoms decrease your risk of acquiring HPV, but this is still not 100 percent effective.

How is it treated? Warts can be treated with laser, freezing, cutting, or several medications that you or your doctor can apply. Often, your immune system will kick in and rid your body of the virus altogether.

Molluscum Contagiosum

Molluscum contagiosum is a skin infection transmitted by intimate contact. You can catch it through sexual contact, nonsexual skin-to-skin touching, or sharing towels.

How do I know if I have it? Symptoms include small, flesh-colored, waxy, dome-shaped bumps that typically appear between two and twelve weeks after exposure. A doctor can determine if you have *Molluscum contagiosum* by evaluating the affected tissue under a microscope.

How is it treated? Your doctor can remove the growths by using chemicals, electrical current, or freezing. Though condoms reduce the risk of *Molluscum contagiosum,* the virus may be in areas not covered by the condom.

Syphilis

Syphilis is caused by a tiny spiral-shaped parasite called *Treponema pallidum.*

How do I know if I have it? The most common symptom is a painless ulcer on your genitals that appears from three weeks to three months after exposure to the infection. The ulcer typically disappears without treatment. Symptoms of advanced syphilis include rashes on the palms of the hands and soles of the feet, mild fever, weight loss, headaches, muscle pain, hair loss, fatigue, and a sore throat. Your doctor can make the diagnosis by conducting blood tests.

How can it be treated? Antibiotics can be used to successfully treat both partners. If caught early, syphilis is fully curable. In late stages, however, damage caused by the disease is irreversible. Using condoms may decrease your risk of infection during vaginal, oral, or anal sex.

Trichomoniasis

Trichomoniasis (trich) is very common. It is caused by the parasite *Trichomonas vaginalis*. Though considered a sexually transmitted infection, trich can be transmitted by nonsexual acts as well.

How do I know if I have it? Trich often causes a heavy, frothy yellow or green vaginal discharge that may be foul smelling. You may also experience severe itching or burning on your vulva and vagina, particularly when you urinate. Your doctor can diagnose you by examining your vaginal discharge under a microscope or by sending your specimen to a laboratory for analysis.

How can it be treated? Your physician can treat trich by prescribing an antibiotic, metronidazole, in a single dose or several days' worth. Your partner also needs to be treated. Using condoms prevents the infection.

Sexy Ways to Be Safer: Ten Tips, Techniques, and Tricks

Create your own "Pleasure Pack." Fill a red satin pouch with condoms of different shapes, colors, textures, and flavors. Japanese condoms, like Kimono, as well as the new Pleasure Plus and Inspiral condoms have a reputation for a higher degree of sensitivity and pleasure, and should be included in every woman's pleasure pack. Complete the pack with a variety of water-based lubricants, including flavored and warming lubes. Keep at your bedside.

Master a new, sensual method of rolling on a condom. One that is certain to get a rise out of him is the "French kissing" technique. With your mouth in the shape of an O, place the condom between your lips. Use your lips and tongue to slowly roll the condom down his penis. Be sure to cover your teeth with your lips to avoid damaging the condom. Practice with a cucumber before springing it on your partner.

Give him a dry hand job while rolling on the condom. Fondle his testicles and stroke the shaft of his penis with one hand. With your other hand, place the lubricated condom on the head of the penis. Now stroke, then roll, then stroke, then roll, until the condom has been completely unrolled on his erect penis.

continued

Make an "Intimacy Travel Pack." Purchase a double-lipstick case. It is the perfect size for one tube of lipstick, two condoms (in case one breaks), and a small travel-size package of your favorite lube. And since you would never be caught without your lipstick, you are always prepared.

To spice up oral sex, buy a variety of flavored latex condoms. You can also tingle your taste buds by smearing a plain latex or polyurethane condom with honey, jelly, chocolate sauce, or a variety of flavored lubes. Just be sure to change to a clean condom before moving on to intercourse to avoid vaginal infections.

Make love with the lights on. Begin lovemaking with a sensual, erotic massage. Besides adding heat to your sex play, it will also give you an opportunity to discreetly inspect the goods before becoming more intimate. Any bumps, drips, sores, or lesions mean that lovemaking must be put on hold until he sees his doctor for an examination.

Go shopping together at your favorite adult store. Most woman-friendly adult stores will allow you to sample lubes, condoms, dental dams, and toys before purchase. The excitement and anticipation of what is to come will put a charge into your sex life. If you don't have an adult store in your town, shop together on-line at Evesgarden.com, Goodvibes.com, or babeland.com.

Try vibrating condom rings. These rings are placed at the base of the condom once it is rolled on the erect penis and

continued

turns an ordinary condom into a sex toy. You can order them online at: *www.condomania.com.*

Lubricate for cunnilingus. Place a few drops of water-based lubricant on your vulva, then cover with a Glyde latex barrier before receiving oral sex or cunnilingus. The lubricant will increase the sensations of oral sex and make it more pleasurable. Place a few drops of flavored lube on the other side to stimulate his taste buds.

Play the grab-bag game. Place a variety of condoms in a bag. Before sex ask your partner to pull out the "condom of the night." You choose the "flavor of the night" by pulling one of a variety of flavored lubes or gels out of a second bag.

More lubrication tricks. Place a couple of drops of water-based lubricant in the tip of the condom before rolling it on. The added lubrication will increase his sensitivity and pleasure. He'll beg for the condom next time.

A Final Word

If there are any words that I would like to leave you with, they would be this: *You are deserving of pleasure. Embrace it!*

Sex is about pleasure—creating, accepting, and sharing it. Sex is not about performance or the goal of orgasm. There is no one right way to have sex or to give and receive pleasure. You must take the time to discover for yourself what makes you feel good. And as you deserve pleasure, you must let your partner know what turns you on and gives you satisfaction.

For a lifetime of pleasure:

- Give yourself permission to be a sexy, sensual, confident, pleasure-seeking woman.
- Take charge of, and responsibility for, your own pleasure.
- Form an erotic relationship with your own body. *Live* in it. Enjoy it.

- Walk around naked and throw away your panties. Free your genitals.
- Feel free to initiate sex, experiment, and have fun.
- Ask for what you want!
- Make your sexual relationship with your partner and your self a priority. Keep it fresh and exciting.
- Write your own sexual script. You and only you make the rules about how you express your sexuality.
- Celebrate and honor whatever pleasure you experience.

Happy Lovemaking!
Hilda Hutcherson, M.D.

Resources

Adult Toys and Erotica
Eve's Garden
1-800-848-3837
www.evesgarden.com

Babes in Toyland
1-800-658-9119
www.babeland.com

Candida Royalle's Femme Products
1-800-456-LOVE
www.royalle.com

Good Vibrations
1-800-buy-vibe
www.goodvibes.com

Grand Opening
(617) 731-2626
www.grandopening.com

Passion Parties
To find a consultant
go to: www.PassionParties.com

Sinclair Intimacy Institute
www.sinclairwholesale.com

Vaginal Dilators
Milex Products, Inc.
(312) 631-6484
www.milexproducts.com/products/other/dilators.asp

Vaginal Weights for Kegel Exercises
www.aswechange.com
www.goodvibes.com or 1-800-buy-vibe
www.bettydodson.com

Further Reading

Barbach, Lonnie Garfield. *For Yourself: The Fulfillment of Female Sexuality.* New York: Doubleday, 1975.

Chalker, Rebecca. *The Clitoral Truth.* New York: Seven Stories Press, 2000.

Crenshaw, Theresa. *The Alchemy of Love and Lust.* New York: Putnam, 1996.

Dodson, Betty. *Sex for One: The Joy of Selfloving.* New York: Crown, 1996.

Douglas, Nik. *Spiritual Sex: Secrets of Tantra from the Ice Age to the New Millennium.* New York: Pocket Books, 1997.

Engel, Beverly. *Raising Your Sexual Self-Esteem: How to Feel Better About Your Sexuality and Yourself.* New York: Ballantine, 1995.

Hatcher, Robert; James Trussel; Felicia Stewart; Anita Nelson; Williard Cates; Felicia Guest; and Deborah Kowal. *Contraceptive Technology.* New York: Ardent Media, 2004.

Hite, Shere. *The Hite Report: A National Study of Female Sexuality.* New York: Macmillan, 1976.

Ladas, Alice; Beverly Whipple; and John Perry. *The G Spot and Other Discoveries About Human Sexualtiy.* New York: Henry Holt, 2005.

Lauman, Edward; John Gagnon; Robert Michael; and Stuart Michaels. *The Social Organization of Sexuality: Sexual Practices in the United States.* Chicago: University of Chicago Press, 1994.

Leiblum, Sandra, and Judith Sachs. *Getting the Sex You Want.* New York: Random House, 2002.

Le Page, Michael. "Orgasms: a real 'turn-off' for women." *New Scientist,* vol. 17, no. 54, 20, June 2005.

LoPiccolo, Joseph, and Charles Lobitz. "The role of masturbation in the treatment of orgasmic dysfunction." *Archives of Sexual Behavior,* vol. 2, no. 2, 163–71, 1972.

Morin, Jack. *Anal Pleasure and Health.* San Francisco: Down There Press, 1998.

Muir, Caroline and Charles. *Tantra: The Art of Conscious Loving.* San Francisco: Mercury House, 1989.

O'Connel, Helen, and John Delancey. "Clitoral anatomy in nulliparous, healthy, premenopausal volunteers using enhanced magnetic resonance imaging." *The Journal of Urology,* vol. 173, 2060–63, June 2005.

Riley, Alan, and Elizabeth Riley. "The effect of Clitstim (Vielle) on sexual response induced by masturbation in female volunteers." *Sexual and Relationship Therapy,* vol. 18, no. 1, 45–52, 2003.

Webster, Richard. *Fung Shui for Love and Romance*. St. Paul: Llewellyn Publications, 1999.

Weiner Davis, Michele. *The Sex Starved Marriage*. New York: Simon & Shuster, 2003.

Whipple, Beverly; Gina Ogden; and Barry R. Komisaruk. "Physiological correlates of imagery-induced orgasm in women." *Archives of Sexual Behavior,* vol. 21, no. 2, 121–33, 1992.

Yucel, Selnuck. "Neuroanatomy of the human female lower genital tract." *The Journal of Urology,* vol. 172, 191–95, July 2004.

Zilbergeld, Bernie. *The New Male Sexuality*. New York: Bantam, 1999.

Index

About the Author

Hilda Hutcherson, M.D., is a monthly columnist for *Glamour* and *Essence* magazines. She is a codirector of the New York Center for Women's Sexual Health at Columbia University Medical Center, and associate professor of obstetrics and gynecology at Columbia University's College of Physicians and Surgeons. A practicing gynecologist for more than twenty years, she has appeared on *The Oprah Winfrey Show,* the *Today* show, and *20/20.* She lives outside New York City with her husband and four children.